EVERY THOUGHT CAPTIVE

HOW RENEWING YOUR MIND CAN CHANGE YOUR LIFE

BIBLE STUDY GUIDE | FIVE SESSIONS

KYLE IDLEMAN

WITH VINCE ANTONUCCI

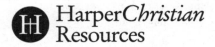

HarperChristian Resources

Every Thought Captive Bible Study Guide
© 2025 by Kyle Idleman

Published in Grand Rapids, Michigan, by HarperChristian Resources. HarperChristian Resources is a registered trademark of HarperCollins Christian Publishing, Inc.

Requests for information should be sent to customercare@harpercollins.com.

ISBN 978-0-310-14066-5 (softcover)
ISBN 978-0-310-17460-8 (ebook)

HarperChristian Resources titles may be purchased in bulk for church, business, fundraising, or ministry use. For information, please e-mail ResourceSpecialist@ChurchSource.com.

First Printing April 2025 / Printed in the United States of America

CONTENTS

A NOTE FROM KYLE

Have you ever felt trapped by negative thoughts? Have you wondered if true transformation is actually possible? Have you ever been frustrated by your inability to break out of self-defeating patterns of behavior? All of us, at some point, find ourselves at war with our minds. We know what we want to do and who we want to be, but our thoughts seem to have a will of their own.

Two thousand years ago, the apostle Paul wrote these powerful words: "We demolish arguments and every pretension that sets itself up against the knowledge of God, and we *take captive every thought to make it obedient to Christ*" (2 Corinthians 10:5, emphasis added). This wasn't just spiritual poetry on Paul's part. Instead, it was a practical command for believers in Christ that still holds profound implications for our lives today.

What Paul understood through divine inspiration, modern neuroscience is now confirming through research: Our brains are incredibly adaptable. Scientists call this *neuroplasticity*—the brain's remarkable ability to form new neural pathways in response to life experiences. This discovery revolutionizes our understanding of mental transformation. It also aligns perfectly with some other powerful words from Paul: "Do not conform to the pattern of this world, but be transformed by the renewing of your mind" (Romans 12:2).

Those persistent negative thoughts that seem to plague you? They are simply well-worn neural pathways that have been created through repetition. But here's the incredible news: They don't have to define you. Through the power of the Holy Spirit, and intentional practice, you can create new thought patterns that align with God's truth and design for your life.

In this study, we will journey together through the intersection of biblical wisdom and neuroscientific discovery. You will learn practical techniques for how to capture those thoughts that don't serve you well and how to replace them with God's life-giving truths. This isn't just about positive thinking—it's about experiencing the profound transformation that comes when you align your mind with the truth of God that has the power to set you free.

Whether you are struggling with anxiety, self-doubt, or any other challenging thought patterns, this study will offer you hope and practical steps on how to move forward. As you explore these principles, you will discover how to cooperate with God's grace and your brain's natural ability to change—creating lasting transformation in your thought life.

Are you ready to begin? Let's jump in and discover together how to take every thought captive and experience the freedom that comes with a transformed mind.

— KYLE IDLEMAN

HOW TO USE THIS GUIDE

The stakes couldn't be higher when it comes to taking our thoughts captive. After all, what we think about shapes our emotions, drives our actions, and ultimately determines the course of our lives. Left unchecked, our thoughts can lead us down paths of destruction or, at best, stagnation and mediocrity. But when we learn to harness the power of our minds, aligning our thoughts with God's truth, we unlock the potential for profound change and abundant living.

This is the purpose of this study—to help you identify toxic thought patterns, interrupt negative mental loops, replace lies with God's truth, implement daily habits to reinforce healthy thought patterns, and cultivate a mindset that leads to peace and purpose. Before you begin, know that there are a few ways you can go through this material. You can experience this study with others in a group (such as a Bible study, Sunday school class, or other gathering), or you can go through the content on your own. Either way, the videos are available to view at any time by following the instructions provided with this study guide.

GROUP STUDY

Each of the sessions in this study are divided into two parts: (1) a group study section, and (2) a personal study section. The group study section provides a basic framework on how to open your time together, get the most out of the video content, and discuss the key ideas that were presented in the teaching. Each session includes the following:

- **Welcome:** A short opening note about the topic of the session for you to read on your own before you meet as a group.
- **Connect:** A few icebreaker questions to get you and your group members thinking about the topic and interacting with each other.

- **Watch:** An outline of the key points covered in each video teaching along with space for you to take notes as you watch each session.
- **Discuss:** Questions to help you and your group reflect on the teaching material presented and apply it to your lives.
- **Respond:** A short personal exercise to help reinforce the key ideas.
- **Pray:** A place for you to record prayer requests and praises for the week.

If you are doing this study in a group, make sure you have your own copy of the study guide so you can write down your thoughts, responses, and reflections in the space provided—and so you have access to the videos via streaming. You will also want to have a copy of the *Every Thought Captive* book, as reading it alongside this guide will provide you with deeper insights. (See the notes at the beginning of each group session and personal study section on which chapters of the book you should read before the next group session.)

Finally, keep these points in mind:

- **Facilitation:** If you are doing this study in a group, you will want to appoint someone to serve as a facilitator. This person will be responsible for starting the video and keeping track of time during discussions and activities. If *you* have been chosen for this role, there are some resources in the back of this guide that can help you lead your group through the study.

- **Faithfulness:** Your group is a place where tremendous growth can happen as you reflect on the Bible, ask questions, and learn what God is doing in other people's lives. For this reason, be fully committed and attend each session so you can build trust and rapport with the other members.

- **Friendship:** The goal of any small group is to serve as a place where people can share, learn about God, and build friendships. So seek to make your group a "safe place." Be honest about your thoughts and feelings, but also listen carefully to everyone else's thoughts, feelings, and opinions. Keep anything personal your group members share in confidence so you can create a community where people can heal, be challenged, and grow spiritually.

If you are going through this study on your own, read the opening Welcome section and reflect on the questions in the Connect section. Watch the video and use the outline provided to help you take notes. Finally, personalize the questions and exercises in the Discuss and Respond sections. Close by recording any requests you want to pray about during the week.

PERSONAL STUDY

The personal study is for you to work through on your own during the week. Each exercise is designed to help you explore the key ideas you uncovered during your group time and delve into passages of Scripture that will help you apply those principles to your life. Go at your own pace, doing a little each day—or tackle the material all at once. Remember to spend a few moments in silence to listen to whatever God might be saying to you.

Note that if you are doing this study as part of a group, and you are unable to finish (or even start) these personal studies for the week, you should still attend the group time. Be assured that you are still wanted and welcome even if you don't have your "homework" done. The group studies and personal studies are intended to help you hear what God wants you to hear and learn how to apply what he is saying to your life. So . . . as you go through this study, be listening for him to speak to you about what it means to *take every thought captive.*

WEEK 1

BEFORE GROUP MEETING	Read the introduction and chapters 1–3 in *Every Thought Captive* Read the Welcome section (page 2)
GROUP MEETING	Discuss the Connect questions Watch the video teaching for session 1 Discuss the questions that follow as a group Do the closing exercise and pray (pages 2–6)
STUDY 1	Complete the personal study (pages 8–11)
STUDY 2	Complete the personal study (pages 12–15)
STUDY 3	Complete the personal study (pages 16–19)
CONNECT & DISCUSS	Connect with one or two group members Discuss the follow-up questions (page 20)
CATCH UP & READ AHEAD (BEFORE WEEK 2 GROUP MEETING)	Read chapters 4–5 in *Every Thought Captive* Complete any unfinished studies (page 21)

CONFORMED OR TRANSFORMED

Therefore, I urge you, brothers and sisters, in view of God's mercy, to offer your bodies as a living sacrifice, holy and pleasing to God—this is your true and proper worship. Do not conform to the pattern of this world, but be transformed by the renewing of your mind. Then you will be able to test and approve what God's will is—his good, pleasing and perfect will.

ROMANS 12:1-2

WELCOME | READ ON YOUR OWN

In a master wood-carver's workshop, every piece of timber holds hidden potential. The artisan sees beyond the exterior to the beauty waiting to emerge. With practiced hands, the master begins removing layers—each cut precise . . . each stroke intentional. Through thousands of careful movements, what was once raw lumber slowly begins to reveal its true nature. Intricate patterns emerge, graceful forms take shape, and rough surfaces become smooth as silk beneath the craftsman's touch.

Our minds work in similar ways. Our thoughts, like that of uncarved wood, are constantly being shaped and refined. Scientists tell us the human has around six thousand thoughts each day.[1] Each one is like another stroke of the carving tool, revealing either the masterpiece within or leaving unwanted gouges in our consciousness.

This is why Paul writes, "Do not conform to the pattern of this world, but be transformed by the renewing of your mind" (Romans 12:2). The world acts like an unskilled hand, hacking at our thoughts without vision or purpose, and our minds can become scarred and misshapen by its crude attempts to form us.

But God, the master Craftsman, offers us a different way. Instead of being hewn by the world's agenda, we can place ourselves under his caring hands. He knows exactly where to cut, precisely how deep to go, and how to perfectly reveal the image he envisions within us. The transformation that he offers isn't quick or easy. Rather, like a fine wood carving, it requires patience, precision, and trust in the artist's vision.

The choice is ours. Will we allow our thoughts to be randomly chipped by the world? Or will we submit them to the careful shaping of the Master's hands?

CONNECT | 10 MINUTES

If you or any of your group members don't know each other, take a few minutes to introduce yourselves. Then discuss one or both of the following questions:

- What do you hope to learn through this study?

- On a scale of 1 (low) to 10 (high), how would you rate your present ability to take your thoughts captive? Explain your response.

WATCH | 25 MINUTES

Watch the video, which you can access by playing the DVD or through streaming (see the instructions provided with this guide). Below is an outline of the key points covered during the teaching. Record any key concepts that stand out to you.

OUTLINE

I. Our minds are constantly being shaped and molded.
   A. Like molten glass, our lives are being shaped by our thoughts (Romans 12:2).
   B. Modern theories of neuroplasticity confirm biblical wisdom (Proverbs 4:23).
   C. The law of cognition states that thoughts determine beliefs, beliefs determine feelings, and feelings determine actions and lifestyle.[2]

II. Exposure can be a powerful force in shaping our thoughts.
   A. Whether we think about our repeated thoughts or not, they are "turning up the heat," each thought a little bit more than the last, to shape us and mold us.
   B. The rule of exposure states that whatever we are exposed to the most shapes our thoughts.[3]
   C. The Bible warns that if we do not determine to take our thoughts captive, then our thoughts will take us captive.

III. *Strongholds* are places in our lives where our thoughts are holding us captive.
   A. Strongholds are formed by ingrained patterns of thinking that are opposed to God's truth.
   B. Strongholds in our minds are like ancient fortresses on high peaks, reinforced with walls of false thinking and protected by lies that seem impenetrable.
   C. If we want to change our lives, these strongholds must fall (2 Corinthians 10:5).

IV. The Bible provides a pathway to transforming our thoughts.
   A. It's not enough to just change our behaviors or address our habits. Behaviors come back. Habits have a way of returning, oftentimes stronger than before.
   B. We must identify our current thought patterns and our mental strongholds. This goes beyond mere behavior modification—we must actually address what is at the root of our thinking patterns.
   C. Active engagement is required: monitoring exposure to negative thoughts, challenging existing thought patterns, and creating new neural pathways.
   D. With God's help, we can create new neural pathways every time we choose to think differently.

NOTES

DISCUSS | 35 MINUTES

Discuss what you just watched by answering the following questions.

1. Take a moment to think about your typical day. What kinds of thoughts tend to dominate your mind? Where do these thoughts primarily come from (media, relationships, work, some other source)? How might these thoughts be shaping who you are becoming?

2. Ask someone to read aloud 1 John 2:15–17. In this passage, we are told not to "love the world or anything in the world." What are some of the ways that the world around you tries to influence your thinking? What are some recent examples of this?

3. The "rule of exposure" states that whatever we are exposed to the most will shape our thoughts the most. How have you witnessed the truth of this rule in your life? Consider the example in the teaching of Seth Godin listening to motivational content for three hours each day. How could you be more intentional about what you expose your mind to?

4. Ask someone to read aloud Ephesians 6:12. Mental strongholds are like fortresses reinforced with walls of false thinking and protected by lies that seem impenetrable. Who does Paul say in this verse is behind these strongholds? What does this reveal about the enemy's intent to keep us locked up in negative patterns of thinking?

5. Transforming our thinking requires a fundamental rewiring of how we process the world around us. This journey begins with monitoring our exposure. What are some of the things that you are exposing your mind to that could potentially be leading you down the wrong path? What are some of the positive voices in your life that you are listening to?

RESPOND | 10 MINUTES

The apostle Paul makes it clear that when it comes to our thoughts, we are not up against flesh and blood but against "the spiritual forces of evil in the heavenly realms" (Ephesians 6:12). Fortunately, God has given us divine weapons to take down enemy strongholds and reclaim the territory of our minds. Take a few minutes on your own to read what Paul says about these weapons in the following passage, and then answer the questions that follow.

> For though we live in the world, we do not wage war as the world does. The weapons we fight with are not the weapons of the world. On the contrary, they have divine power to demolish strongholds. We demolish arguments and every pretension that sets itself up against the knowledge of God.
>
> 2 CORINTHIANS 10:3–5

What does Paul mean when he says that we do not wage war as the world does?

What are we specifically instructed in this passage to demolish in our lives?

What thoughts have you been confronted with recently that "[set themselves] up against the knowledge of God"? Why is it so critical to know God's truth?

PRAY | 10 MINUTES

As you close this session, pray together for transformation through the renewal of your minds. Pray about any strongholds that need to be demolished and the new thought patterns you want to develop. Ask God for wisdom in managing your exposure to various influences and in being intentional about what shapes your thinking. Before closing, write down any specific prayer requests related to mental strongholds that group members want to focus on this week.

PERSONAL STUDY

In this opening session, you were introduced to the topic of this study: *becoming the person you want to become by winning the battle for your mind*. The Bible is the best resource for information on this topic. So, in the personal study portion of each session, you will be taking a deeper look at specific passages and principles in God's Word that are the most helpful in taking every thought captive. As you work through each of these exercises, be sure to write down your responses to the questions, as you will be given a few minutes to share your insights and key takeaways at the start of the next session. If you are reading *Every Thought Captive* alongside this study, first review the introduction and chapters 1–3 in the book.

THE BATTLE FOR YOUR MIND

Thousands of thoughts pass through your mind each day. Each one leaves an impression, like a fingerprint on soft clay. Some are fleeting—barely noticed and quickly forgotten. Others repeat themselves, wearing deeper grooves into your thinking patterns with each pass. Like water flowing over rock, these repetitive thoughts gradually carve channels in your mind, creating paths of least resistance that your future thoughts will naturally follow. This process begins in childhood and continues throughout your life, shaping not just your thought patterns but also your emotional responses, decision-making habits, and even your personality.

Scientists call this phenomenon *neuroplasticity*. When researchers observe the brain through advanced imaging, they can actually see these neural pathways strengthen or weaken based on use.[4] Every worry we entertain, every truth we meditate on, and every lie we believe creates neural pathways that become our mind's default routes. When we repeatedly think about failure, our brain becomes wired for defeat. When we constantly replay past hurts, our mind becomes programmed for pain. Even our stress responses and emotional resilience are shaped by these well-worn mental paths.

Here is where science catches up to what the Bible has always taught: These pathways aren't permanent. Paul states that you can be "transformed by the renewing of your mind" (Romans 12:2). The Greek word he uses is *metamorphoo*, which is a complete restructuring from the inside out. Every time you choose to redirect your thoughts, to challenge old patterns with God's truth, you're literally rewiring your brain. Each time you take a thought captive and make it obedient to Christ, you're carving new channels for God's truth to flow. This process requires intentional effort and repetition, but the brain's remarkable plasticity means that no thought pattern is too deeply entrenched to change.

The world is pressing you into its mold, one thought at a time. From social media algorithms to advertising strategies, you face sophisticated systems designed to influence your behaviors. But God offers a different mold—one that shapes you into the image of Christ. The choice lies before you: *Whose pattern will you allow your thoughts to follow?* The answer to this question will shape not just your mind but also your entire life.

1. Read Romans 12:1–2. What do these verses say about the importance of your thought life? How would you define what it means to "be transformed by the renewing of your mind"?

2. One ancient author advised, "Be careful how you think; your life is shaped by your thoughts. Never say anything that isn't true. Have nothing to do with lies and misleading words" (Proverbs 4:23–24 GNT). How do you react to this idea that your life is shaped by your thoughts? What does this say about the importance of speaking the truth to yourself and others?

In psychology there's a principle called "the law of cognition." Simply stated, what you think about determines who you become. More specifically, what you think about determines what you believe; what you believe determines how you feel; how you feel determines what you do and how you live. Let's say that in reverse so we don't miss the significance: What I do is determined by how I feel; how I feel is determined by what I believe; what I believe is determined by what I think about. So the question is, "What do I think about?" Because what you think about matters, even if you don't think it matters. . . . Either you take your thoughts captive, or they will take you captive.[5]

3. The law of cognition states that what you think about determines who you become—and this is true regardless of whether you think it is true! Take a moment to consider your current thought patterns. What kind of person are they leading you to become in these areas?

Relationally:	Spiritually:

Emotionally:	Professionally:

4. Read Romans 8:5–8. What does Paul say about the importance of your thoughts? What does he say is the result of having a mind that is governed by the Holy Spirit?

Being transformed by the renewing of our minds is not something that happens automatically or accidently; it takes intentionality and effort. This is not a stroll in the park; it's a tug-of-war. Our spiritual formation is *counter*transformation. We battle against our flesh, our old sinful habits, the world we live in, our enemy who rules over it, and the mold that always seems to be squeezing us.[6] If we don't choose transformation, we won't just sit in neutral; we will be left to the persistent molding of the world, dragged in the opposite direction of who we wanted to become.[7]

5. Close this study by actually tracking some of your thoughts today. Based on your best guess / rough estimate, what percentage of your thoughts fell into each category?

Worries, anxieties, and fears:

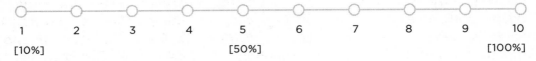

1	2	3	4	5	6	7	8	9	10
[10%]				[50%]					[100%]

Self-criticism:

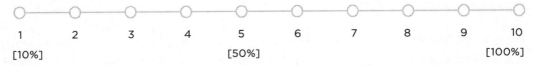

1	2	3	4	5	6	7	8	9	10
[10%]				[50%]					[100%]

Self-doubt:

1	2	3	4	5	6	7	8	9	10
[10%]				[50%]					[100%]

God's truth about you:

1	2	3	4	5	6	7	8	9	10
[10%]				[50%]					[100%]

THE FORTRESS WITHIN

In ancient warfare, a stronghold was more than just a fortress. It was also a place of refuge, often built on the highest peak with walls so thick they seemed impenetrable. When enemies attacked, the people in the surrounding countryside would retreat to these strongholds, believing themselves safe behind the walls of solid stone. The architecture of these fortresses was precise, with each stone placed to create an integrated defense system. Watchtowers provided clear sight lines in all directions, and hidden chambers stored provisions. These strongholds weren't built in a day—they were the result of years, sometimes generations, of meticulous construction.

We build similar fortresses in our minds. The hurts, disappointments, and fears that we experience over the years construct mental strongholds—thought patterns so deeply entrenched they seem like permanent structures. These are not just bad habits or negative thinking but are *fortified* belief systems that stand in opposition to God's truth. Like ancient strongholds, they become places where lies take refuge, deception feels like safety, and wrong thinking seems like protection. Each painful experience adds another stone to the wall, until these fortresses of falsehood become as familiar as home.

Maybe it's a stronghold of unworthiness, built from childhood rejection. Perhaps it's a fortress of anxiety, reinforced by years of what-if scenarios. Or it could be a citadel of addiction, where past failures have convinced us that change is impossible. Just as the inhabitants of ancient cities would retreat to strongholds during attacks, so we often retreat to these familiar places when life challenges us. We may even take pride in our strongholds, viewing them as wisdom gained from experience rather than recognizing them as prisons that limit our growth.

Paul tells us something revolutionary in 2 Corinthians 10:3–5: Through Christ, we have divine power to demolish these strongholds. This demolition isn't a gentle process. It requires aggressive action against entrenched lies, sustained assault on false beliefs, and the courage to stand exposed as our defensive walls crumble. The question isn't whether we have mental strongholds—we all do. The question is whether we will let them stand or allow God's truth to tear them down, stone by stone, until we stand free in the open spaces of his grace.

1. Take another look at 2 Corinthians 10:3–5, which you examined during this week's group time. What does Paul specifically say about each of the following?

The nature of the battle:

The weapons you have been given to use:

The goal of the fight:

2. Read Psalm 18:1–6. How do these verses redefine what should be our true stronghold? How does it contrast with the harmful strongholds in our minds?

A helpful way to identify a stronghold in your life is to think about an area in which you feel stuck. You're not sure *why* you're stuck; you just know you're stuck. As you think about that area, ask yourself, *Is there a lie I'm believing?* When you believe a lie, you give it the power of truth in your life. . . . Little lies can make little changes in your life. And if that's true, wouldn't big lies make big changes? When you believe a lie, you give it the power of truth in your life. The way you think determines how you live. Generational strongholds pass down broken thinking from one generation to the next.[8]

3. Consider what might be some of your personal strongholds—areas where the enemy has infiltrated and taken ground. What lies have you fortified in the following areas?

Lies about your purpose:

Lies about your security:

Lies about your identity:

4. Choose one of these mental strongholds that you identified. Examine it using this analysis:

What is the foundation of this lie?
What are the walls that protect it?
What truth can demolish it?

5. Proverbs 21:22 gives some practical advice if you ever find yourself having to attack a city: "A wise man scales the city of the mighty and brings down the stronghold in which they trust" (ESV). The idea is that if you attack a city, get the stronghold; because if you don't, the city will reestablish itself. In the same way, if you want to change your life, it's not enough to change the behavior—you have to take down the stronghold. Look again at the mental stronghold you identified. What practical steps are needed to truly take it down?

GUARDING THE GATES

J. K. Rowling's original manuscript for Harry Potter was rejected by twelve different publishing houses. One agent even warned her, "You do realize, you will never make a fortune out of writing children's books?" Today, the Harry Potter series has sold more than six hundred million copies worldwide, making it the bestselling book series in history.[9] So, what enabled Rowling to go on in spite of all those rejections?

In her own words, "I pinned my first rejection letter to my kitchen wall, because it gave me something in common with all my fave writers!" She also determined not to give up until every single publisher turned her down . . . though she feared that would happen.[10] In other words, Rowling determined not to view her rejections as *failures* but as something that made her a *member* of a prestigious group of fellow writers. Rather than allowing those rejection letter to derail her dreams, she used them as fuel to fan the flames.

Our minds are like gardens—whatever we plant and water will grow. Left untended, weeds of doubt and fear will take root. But with care, we can cultivate an environment where truth and wisdom flourish. Think about your daily mental diet. If you constantly expose yourself to fear-based news, your anxiety grows. If you immerse yourself in comparison-driven social media, your insecurity flourishes. If you surround yourself with cynicism, your hope withers. Each exposure adds another drop of water to that particular plant in your mental garden.

But the reverse is equally true. When you expose yourself to God's truth, faith grows. When you immerse yourself in worship, peace flourishes. When you surround yourself with people who are wise, discernment develops. When you meditate on Scripture, your understanding deepens. This isn't about positive thinking. It's about strategic exposure to the truth of God that will transform your heart and your mind.

This principle of "selective exposure" challenges us to audit our mental intake. What voices do we listen to most? What messages do we repeatedly expose ourselves to? What images and ideas do we allow to take up residence in our minds? Just as a financial advisor would tell us to track our spending, perhaps it's time to track our mental consumption.

1. Read Philippians 4:8–9. Evaluate your daily exposure against each of the following criteria. What percentage of what you see, read, or hear would you say is the following?

True:	_____%		Noble:	_____%
Right:	_____%		Pure:	_____%
Lovely:	_____%		Admirable:	_____%
Excellent:	_____%		Praiseworthy:	_____%

In Hebrew culture during Solomon's time, the heart and mind would have been thought of interchangeably. *Leb* is the Hebrew word translated "heart." One definition renders it as "the inner man, mind, will, heart. . . ."[11] The team of scholars who translated Solomon's original Hebrew in Proverbs 4:23 chose "guard your heart," but they could just as well have translated it "guard your mind" or "guard your thoughts." . . . If your life is shaped by your thoughts, and your thoughts reflect whatever you're exposed to the most, then what you are exposing your mind to is molding you.[12]

2. Read Proverbs 4:20–27. Why should guarding your heart (or mind) be a priority? What is the importance of giving "careful thought to the paths for your feet"?

3. Notice in this passage that Solomon (writing from the perspective of a father giving advice to his son) also advises his readers to guard their ears (verses 20–21), their mouths (verse 24), and their eyes (verse 25). Your ears and your eyes are the gateway to your heart, while your mouth is a representation of what is in your heart (see Luke 6:45). Given this, take a moment to consider how effectively you are guarding each of these in your life.

Worries, anxieties, and fears:

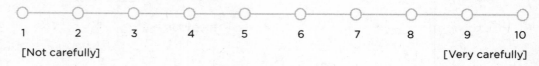

Worries, anxieties, and fears:
1   2   3   4   5   6   7   8   9   10
[Not carefully]   [Very carefully]

How carefully do you guard whom you listen to?

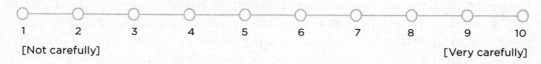

1   2   3   4   5   6   7   8   9   10
[Not carefully]   [Very carefully]

How carefully do you guard what you look at?

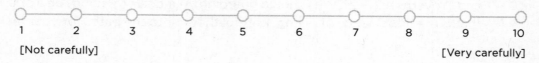

1   2   3   4   5   6   7   8   9   10
[Not carefully]   [Very carefully]

How carefully do you guard what you say to others?

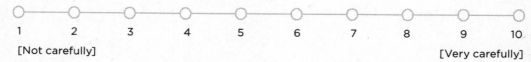

1   2   3   4   5   6   7   8   9   10
[Not carefully]   [Very carefully]

If we change our input, it will change our output. . . . You say, *I want to be humble*. Start by checking your input. If it's constant consumerism, which always tells you to put yourself and your needs first, that you are entitled and the center of your world, it will be extremely difficult to grow in humility. You say, *I want to be holy, to walk in purity*. What's your input? What images are you putting in your mind? Some Christians read the Bible and shake their heads in disgust at Solomon because he had a thousand wives, but they're seeking out more sexual images in a week than Solomon saw in his entire life. If that's your input, don't expect to grow in holiness. Your input will come out in your life, one way or another. What you are exposed to will shape your thoughts.[13]

4. Read 1 Peter 5:5–7. What should you do if you want to be humble? What input might you need to change in your life if you want to witness that output?

5. Now read Psalm 119:9–16. What should you do if you want to stay on the "path of purity"? What input might you need to change to see that output?

CONNECT AND DISCUSS

Take time today to connect with a group member and talk about some of the insights from this session. Use any of the prompts below to help guide your discussion.

Which elements of this session about how your life is being shaped by your thoughts most caught your attention? Why those particular elements?

Why is exposure—what you choose to open yourself to—such a force in shaping your thoughts?

What did you learn from this session about the power of strongholds in your mind and the hold they can have over you?

In what ways are you encouraged to know that real change is possible if you approach it through thought transformation rather than behavior modification?

What thought patterns in your life are you realizing need transformation?

CATCH UP AND READ AHEAD

Use this time to go back and complete any of the study and reflection questions from previous days that you weren't able to finish. Make a note below of any revelations you've had and reflect on any growth or personal insights you've gained.

Read chapters 4–5 in *Every Thought Captive* before the next group session. Use the space below to make note of anything in those chapters that inspires you, stands out to you, or encourages you.

WEEK 2

BEFORE GROUP MEETING	Read chapters 4–5 in *Every Thought Captive* Read the Welcome section (page 24)
GROUP MEETING	Discuss the Connect questions Watch the video teaching for session 2 Discuss the questions that follow as a group Do the closing exercise and pray (pages 24–28)
STUDY 1	Complete the personal study (pages 30–33)
STUDY 2	Complete the personal study (pages 34–37)
STUDY 3	Complete the personal study (pages 38–41)
CONNECT & DISCUSS	Connect with one or two group members Discuss the follow-up questions (page 42)
CATCH UP & READ AHEAD (BEFORE WEEK 3 GROUP MEETING)	Read chapters 6–8 in *Every Thought Captive* Complete any unfinished studies (page 43)

SESSION TWO

THE PATTERN OF DISTRACTION

[AND INSECURITY]

But Martha was distracted by all the preparations that had to be made. She came to him and asked, "Lord, don't you care that my sister has left me to do the work by myself? Tell her to help me!" "Martha, Martha," the Lord answered, "you are worried and upset about many things, but few things are needed—or indeed only one. Mary has chosen what is better."

LUKE 10:40-42

WELCOME | READ ON YOUR OWN

Stand at any busy downtown intersection and you'll witness the intricate dance of urban life—honking horns, flashing billboards, street vendors calling out. Each stimulus competes for mental bandwidth, creating a sensory tapestry designed to catch our gaze. It's civilization orchestrated to captivate and consume.

But this isn't just a city scene—it's a mirror of our daily mental landscape. Like those bustling streets, the world bombards us with notifications, alerts, and streams of content, each carefully engineered to hijack our neural circuitry. Each touch of our phone and moment of screen time reinforces neural pathways that make distraction our default mode and gradually rewires our brains for perpetual fragmentation.

We find a timeless illustration of this battle for our attention in the story of Martha and Mary. While Martha rushed about, her sister, Mary, chose to give Jesus her undivided focus. Martha's distractions weren't sinful—they were good acts of service—but they kept her from experiencing what Jesus said "is better." This is the danger of distraction. Often, it's not *bad* things that fragment our attention but *good* things that keep us from the *best* thing. Like Martha, we can find ourselves upset about many things and miss the one thing that matters most. Our scattered focus becomes not just a habit but also a shield against deeper engagement.

God invites us to a different pattern—one of focused presence and intentional living where silence and solitude become spaces for transformation. The choice is ours. Will we let our minds be shaped by the chaos of constant distraction? Or will we cultivate the discipline of undivided attention to what matters most?

CONNECT | 10 MINUTES

If you or any of your group members don't know each other, take a few minutes to introduce yourselves. Then discuss one or both of the following questions:

- What is something that resonated with you in last week's personal study that you would like to share with the group?

- What would you say distracts you the most—your phone, thoughts about work, the news, television, or something else?

WATCH | 25 MINUTES

Now watch the video for this session. Below is an outline of the main points covered during the teaching. Record any key concepts that stand out to you.

OUTLINE

I. We are bombarded by thought patterns that are reinforced by our culture.
   A. Neuroscience shows that repeated thoughts strengthen neural connections.[14]
   B. These patterns shape our perceptions, emotions, and actions without us even realizing it.
   C. This is especially true with the pattern of distraction.

II. Distraction has become a huge problem in our modern culture.
   A. The average person touches their phone 2,617 times a day[15] and spends an average of seven hours each day on their screens.[16]
   B. This pattern of distraction impacts other negative thought patterns today.
   C. We cannot navigate our spiritual lives with divided attention and focus.

III. The story of Martha and Mary can help us understand how Jesus wants us to handle distractions (Luke 10:38–42).
   A. Martha is confronted with the unexpected arrival of Jesus and his disciples. She quickly sees all the things that need to happen for her to be a good host.
   B. Martha soon becomes distracted with the preparations. Meanwhile, her sister, Mary, chooses to sit at Jesus' feet and listen to all that he says.
   C. Jesus didn't say what Martha was doing was bad—she was actually being selfless—but she was missing out on experiencing what was *better.*

IV. Giving in to the pattern of destruction comes at a cost.
   A. Many video games come with a countdown clock that lets the player know how much time is left.
   B. We need to give our attention to the things that God wants for us, because we only have a limited amount of time in this life (Psalm 90:12; James 4:14).
   C. If we don't break free from the pattern of distraction, it will keep us captive.

V. Some practical strategies for breaking free from the pattern of distraction:
   A. Sacred pause: Pause and ask, "Is this getting me closer to God's purposes?"
   B. Pattern interrupts: Set times when you will shut down the distractions.
   C. Attention training: Devote undistracted time to prayer and Bible reading.
   D. Find a friend: Find someone who will help you stay focused.
   E. Measure what matters: Track your growth when you stay focused on God.

NOTES

DISCUSS | 35 MINUTES

Discuss what you just watched by answering the following questions.

1. There are many benefits that come with our phones. We can quickly contact loved ones, access important information (like driving directions), and save time with all the apps that come with them. But there is no doubt that phones have contributed to increased levels of distraction. If you are feeling bold, take a moment to check your screen time. What patterns do you notice? How might these patterns be affecting your spiritual life?

2. Ask someone to read aloud the full story of Martha and Mary found in Luke 10:38–42. What similarities do you see between Martha's distractions and your own? What are some of the "good things" you are doing that might be distracting you from the "better things"?

3. Notice in the story that when Jesus arrived for a visit, Mary "sat at the Lord's feet listening to what he said" (verse 39). If Jesus were to visit your home today, what would he observe about your priorities and use of time? What one change might he lovingly suggest?

4. Ask someone to read aloud James 4:13–15. What does this passage say about the amount of time we have been given on this earth? How might a greater awareness of just how limited our time is in the here and now change how we handle distractions?

5. Take a moment to review the list of strategies presented in the teaching on how to break free from the pattern of distraction. Which of these strategies would be the most helpful to implement in your life? Which of these strategies would be the most challenging for you?

RESPOND | 10 MINUTES

In our hyperconnected world, it is tragically easy to sleepwalk through life, allowing precious moments to slip away while we are absorbed in lesser things. Like children chasing butterflies past a chest of gold, we often miss divine appointments and kingdom opportunities that are right in front of us because we are distracted by the glittering (but ultimately insignificant) demands of modern life. Take a few minutes to read the following words from Paul on the urgency of staying focused on the things of God, and then answer the questions that follow.

> Everything exposed by the light becomes visible—and everything that is illuminated becomes a light. This is why it is said: "Wake up, sleeper, rise from the dead, and Christ will shine on you." Be very careful, then, how you live—not as unwise but as wise, making the most of every opportunity, because the days are evil. Therefore do not be foolish, but understand what the Lord's will is.
>
> **EPHESIANS 5:13-17**

What opportunities might you be missing due to patterns of distraction?

When are you most vulnerable to distraction? What triggers these moments?

What would it look like for you to "sit at Jesus' feet" in today's world? How might doing so help you to better discern "what the Lord's will is"?

PRAY | 10 MINUTES

Pray together about breaking free from patterns of distraction. Be honest about your struggles with maintaining focus and ask for God's help in creating new patterns for your life. Pray especially for wisdom to distinguish between good things and better things. Before closing, write down any specific prayer requests from the group related to attention and focus.

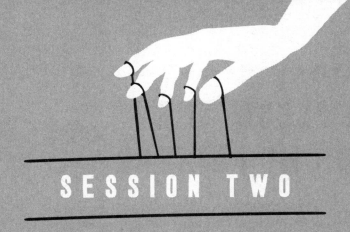

SESSION TWO

PERSONAL STUDY

In the first session, you covered several foundational truths about how to take every thought captive and how to protect your heart and mind. In this session, you began to examine what Paul calls "the pattern of this world" by looking at the dangers of *distraction* and how that particular pattern represents an attack from the enemy against your mind. In this personal study, you will take a deeper look at what Paul means by *patterns*, explore the pattern of distraction in more detail, and also take a look at the pattern of insecurity. As you work through these exercises, again write down your responses to the questions, as you will be given a few minutes to share your insights and key takeaways at the start of the next session. If you are reading *Every Thought Captive* alongside this study, first review chapters 4–5 in the book.

FOLLOW THE RIGHT PATTERN

In the first session, we examined how Paul warns us not to "conform to the pattern of this world" (Romans 12:2). Interestingly, Paul doesn't use the Greek word for *pattern* that often appears in the New Testament. This word, *tupos*, is translated not only as *pattern* but also as *example*, *model*, or *type*. For instance, *tupos* describes the "pattern" of the nail prints on Jesus' hands (see John 20:25). Paul uses it when he asks believers to walk according to his "example" (see Philippians 3:17) and describes how Adam was a "type" of Christ (see Romans 5:14).

The Greek verb that Paul employs in Romans 12:2 is *suschematizo*. This term means "to conform one's self (one's mind and character) to another's pattern."[17] It is used only one other time in the New Testament, when Peter instructs his readers to "not conform [*suschematizo*] to the evil desires you had when you lived in ignorance" (1 Peter 1:14). In each case, the warning is for us to not allow this "age" or "world" to determine how our lives will be shaped. Instead, we are to allow the presence of God and his kingdom to press in on us so we will be shaped into the likeness of Christ.

If you've ever taken on a sewing project, you know how a pattern works. The pattern provides a guide on how to sew the garment to the desired size and fit. It typically includes a set of pieces, drawn flat, that you lay out over the fabric. By following the pattern, you can be sure that you are cutting the pieces to the right size and in the correct order, and as long as you follow the pattern for *your* project, things should go well. However, if you mix in the pattern for a different project—like the pattern for a shirt when you are making a pair of pants—you won't get the result you want. You will end up with something different than you had planned.

The same is true when it comes to our minds. As long as we are conforming to God's shaping process and following his exact pattern, we will stay on track in our quest to become more like Christ. But if we start mixing in other patterns from the world—like patterns of insecurity, distraction, offense, pleasure, and despair—we will end up with something far different from our desired goal. It just comes down to whom we will allow to shape our minds.

1. Read 1 John 2:15–17. What is the "world"? How can you know if something is coming from the world rather than from your heavenly Father?

The thoughts we think are not isolated events; they create intricate neural pathways in our brains that shape our lives in predictable ways. These pathways, or thought patterns, become the lenses through which we interpret the world and respond to it. . . . The "pattern of this world" that Paul refers to in Romans 12:2 can be understood as the pervasive thought patterns reinforced by our culture. Neuroscientific research has shown that repeated thoughts strengthen neural connections, making these patterns increasingly automatic and difficult to break. These culturally reinforced thought patterns can become deeply ingrained, shaping our perceptions, emotions, and actions, often without our conscious awareness.[18]

2. A modern definition of the word *pattern* is "a particular way in which something usually happens or is done."[19] Patterns can be helpful in establishing routines and doing repetitive tasks without giving much thought to them. Take a moment to consider some of the patterns that you have created to manage your day and write them in the table below.

Morning patterns
Noontime patterns

Afternoon patterns
Evening patterns

3. Read Philippians 3:17–21. What pattern were the believers in Philippi to follow? What reasons does Paul provide in instructing them to follow this pattern?

4. Now turn to 1 Timothy 4:11–14. What pattern (or example) was Timothy to set for the church? What was Timothy to do to help him set the right pattern?

Our minds can easily be conformed to ways of thinking that lead us away from God's best for us. But God doesn't leave us there. He offers us a way out. As the apostle Paul writes in Romans 12:2, "Be transformed by the renewing of your mind." This transformation isn't just a nice idea or a spiritual metaphor; it's a practical reality that we can experience in our daily lives. We can have our minds renewed—if we actively participate in this transformative process—and reshape our neural pathways, leading to lasting change in our thoughts, emotions, and behaviors.[20]

5. Lasting change in our thoughts, emotions, and behaviors is possible in Christ. Who is someone in your life today who needs this reassurance? What are some practical steps that you will take today to reach out to that person and encourage him or her?

Person in your life who needs this reassurance:

Practical steps you will take to reach out and encourage that person today:

THE DISHARMONY OF DIVIDED ATTENTION

Imagine sitting in a concert hall as an orchestra tunes their instruments. The musicians focus intently on their pitch, listening carefully so they will blend with those around them. The air vibrates with possibility as the notes begin to coalesce into something greater. Now imagine if half the violinists were checking their phones and the brass section was scrolling social media. The result would be a cacophony instead of harmony. Yet this is exactly how many of us try to navigate our spiritual, emotional, and relational lives—with scattered focus.

Paul warns about this kind of divided attention. "Be very careful, then, how you live," he writes in Ephesians 5:15-16, "not as unwise but as wise, making the most of every opportunity." The word translated as *careful* in Greek (*akribós*) carries the connotation of accuracy, precision, and exactness—the kind of attention required of a musician to create something beautiful. This careful living isn't just about avoiding mistakes; it's about crafting a life of purpose and meaning, note by deliberate note.

Every note we play in life, whether we realize it or not, contributes to a larger symphony. Our daily decisions, responses to others, and presence all become part of the grand composition of our lives. When we try to navigate life's important moments with divided attention, we risk not just hitting wrong notes but also missing out on the very melody that God has composed for us. Just as no orchestra could perform a masterpiece while its members were distracted by their devices, so we cannot effectively pursue our calling, nurture our relationships, or deepen our faith while our attention is fragmented across a thousand different distractions.

Like musicians who must tune out the noise around them to focus on their part in the composition, we, too, must learn to filter out the constant buzz of notifications and demands that threaten to pull us off-key. The most moving performances come when every musician is fully present, fully engaged, and perfectly attuned to both their individual part and the collective whole. The same is true of the "performance" that constitutes our lives.

1. It's time to take a brief inventory of your relationships. Think about each of the following areas of your life. How would you rate how present you typically are in these areas?

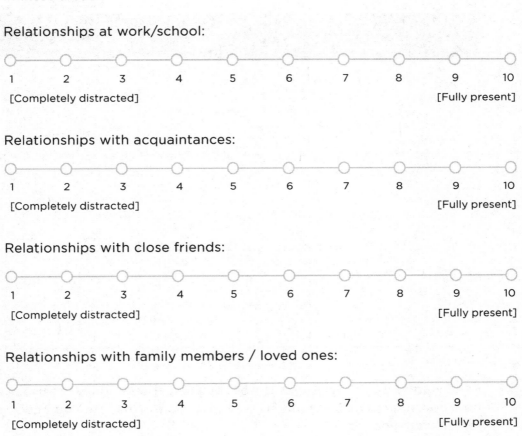

Relationships at work/school:

1   2   3   4   5   6   7   8   9   10

[Completely distracted]   [Fully present]

Relationships with acquaintances:

1   2   3   4   5   6   7   8   9   10

[Completely distracted]   [Fully present]

Relationships with close friends:

1   2   3   4   5   6   7   8   9   10

[Completely distracted]   [Fully present]

Relationships with family members / loved ones:

1   2   3   4   5   6   7   8   9   10

[Completely distracted]   [Fully present]

We incur all kinds of costs from being distracted, but perhaps the most insidious (but often inconspicuous) cost is to our spiritual lives. Theologian Ronald Rolheiser wrote (back in 1999, before the onset of social media and streaming services) that we "are distracting ourselves into spiritual oblivion. . . ."[21] The point is not to regard the internet, social media, TV, video games, and our phones as evil in and of themselves, but to understand that they can all be deadly weapons in the hands of Satan.[22]

2. Consider three recent conversations that you've had with loved ones. How present were you in those conversations? How did your presence/distance impact that conversation?

Situation	How present were you?	What impact did this have?
1.		
2.		
3.		

3. Read Matthew 6:24. While Jesus was speaking about money in this passage, how does this principle apply to your attention? What are you choosing to "serve" with your focus?

4. Now turn to Luke 8:5–15. Focus especially on the seed that fell among the thorns in Jesus' parable (verses 7, 14). What might be some of the "thorns" (distractions) that are choking out spiritual growth in your life? Take a few minutes to list them below.

Among many other negative things, the pattern of distractions leads to *fragmented conversations*. Our interactions are constantly interrupted, breaking the flow of dialogue and connection. However, there's a silver lining. The bar for attentiveness has been set so low that any effort to be fully present can make a significant impact. When we give someone our undivided attention, free from distractions, we communicate a level of value they may not be accustomed to receiving.[23]

5. Paul writes in Philippians 2:3–4 that you are to "value others above yourselves, not looking to your own interests but . . . to the interests of the others." One of the ways you do this is by being fully present with others. Choose one important relationship or activity today where you will commit to being fully present. This means putting your phone away, turning off notifications, and giving your complete attention to that person or task. Write below how this focused attention affected the quality of your experience and relationship.

TRADING PERFORMANCE FOR PRESENCE

Think about children learning to swim. At first, they cling desperately to the pool's edge, certain they will sink if they let go. Their fear isn't just about the water—it's about trusting something they can't see to hold them up. Our insecurities work the same way. We cling to what feels safe—our accomplishments, others' approval, carefully maintained appearances—afraid that if we let go, we will sink into our inadequacies.

Modern life has only amplified these fears. We obsess over professional achievements. We count likes and followers as measures of our worth. We craft perfect online personas while privately wrestling with thoughts like, *Everyone else has it figured out*, or, *I'm falling behind*. It's as if we're trying to build towers of self-worth on foundations of sand, watching anxiously as each new wave threatens to wash them away.

God offers a different approach. He tells us the answer to our insecurity isn't found in becoming more confident in ourselves but in becoming more confident in his presence. When David faced Goliath, his confidence didn't come from comparing his height to the giant's or through analyzing his combat skills. Instead, he declared, "The LORD who rescued me from the paw of the lion and the paw of the bear will rescue me" (1 Samuel 17:37).

This truth echoes throughout Scripture. When Jeremiah protested that he was too young to be a prophet, God didn't list his qualifications. Instead, he promised, "I am with you" (Jeremiah 1:8). When Peter began to sink after walking on water, Jesus didn't give him swimming lessons. He reached out his hand (see Matthew 14:31).

Paul captures this paradox perfectly when he writes, "When I am weak, then I am strong" (2 Corinthians 12:10). Our transformation comes not by embracing our own sufficiency but in embracing Christ's sufficiency in us. True security is built on his unchanging presence—a foundation that remains steady even when everything else seems to shift beneath our feet.

1. Read 1 Samuel 17:32–37. How did David respond when King Saul said he was too young and inexperienced to fight Goliath? What evidence did David provide of God's faithfulness?

2. Turn to Psalm 23:1–6. What confidence does David, the author of this psalm, have that enabled him to "fear no evil" even when was in "the darkest valley"? What security did David say he found in the Lord when he was in the presence of his enemies?

The pattern of insecurity typically looks something like this: (1) caring excessively about what others think; (2) comparing ourselves unfavorably to others; (3) capitulating to negative thoughts and critical self-talk. As we expose the pattern of insecurity in our thinking, we'll see that it typically begins with excessively caring about others' opinions, which leads us to constantly compare ourselves to those around us. This comparison inevitably falls short, causing us to capitulate to negative self-talk and external pressures. This capitulation then reinforces our concern about others' opinions, and we find ourselves trapped in this cyclical pattern.[24]

3. Think about this pattern in your life. How susceptible are you to the following?

Caring excessively about what others think:

○—○—○—○—○—○—○—○—○—○
1   2   3   4   5   6   7   8   9   10

[Infrequently]   [Excessively]

Comparing yourself unfavorably to others:

○—○—○—○—○—○—○—○—○—○
1   2   3   4   5   6   7   8   9   10

[Infrequently]   [Excessively]

Capitulating to negative thoughts and critical self-talk:

○—○—○—○—○—○—○—○—○—○
1   2   3   4   5   6   7   8   9   10

[Infrequently]   [Excessively]

4. Paul wrote, "Am I now trying to win the approval of human beings, or of God? Or am I trying to please people? If I were still trying to please people, I would not be a servant of Christ" (Galatians 1:10). Look at your responses to the thought patterns above. How might the pattern of insecurity be undermining your effectiveness as a servant of Christ?

Breaking the insecurity loop isn't about mustering up more self-confidence or repeating positive mantras; it's about tuning your ear to hear the voice of your heavenly Father. It's about allowing his words of love and affirmation to sink deep into your heart and overwrite the lies of insecurity with the truth of your identity in him. Let his words of love and affirmation become the new soundtrack of your mind. You are loved. You are valued. You are enough—not because of anything you've done or failed to do, but because as a follower of Jesus, you are a child of God.[25]

5. David was confident in facing Goliath not because of his own strength but because of God's strength in him. Think of a time when you felt secure in God's presence despite external uncertainties. What made that moment different from times when you have relied on your own capabilities? How might you carry that experience into current challenges?

What made this moment different from times you relied on yourself:

How you could carry this experience into current challenges:

CONNECT AND DISCUSS

Take time today to connect with a group member and talk about some of the insights from this session. Use any of the prompts below to help guide your discussion.

Which elements of this session about patterns of distraction and insecurity caught your attention the most? Why those particular elements?

In what ways do you most fall prey to the pattern of distraction?

What situations tend to trigger the pattern of insecurity in your life?

How do you see the patterns of distraction and insecurity negatively impacting your relationship with God?

In what ways do you see the patterns of distraction and insecurity negatively impacting your relationships with the people who matter most?

CATCH UP AND READ AHEAD

Use this time to go back and complete any of the study and reflection questions from previous days that you weren't able to finish. Make a note below of any revelations you've had and reflect on any growth or personal insights you've gained.

Read chapters 6–8 in *Every Thought Captive* before the next group session. Use the space below to make note of anything in those chapters that inspires you, stands out to you, or encourages you.

WEEK 3

CATCH UP AND READ AHEAD

BEFORE GROUP MEETING	Read chapters 6–8 in *Every Thought Captive* Read the Welcome section (page 46)
GROUP MEETING	Discuss the Connect questions Watch the video teaching for session 3 Discuss the questions that follow as a group Do the closing exercise and pray (pages 46–50)
STUDY 1	Complete the personal study (pages 52–55)
STUDY 2	Complete the personal study (pages 56–59)
STUDY 3	Complete the personal study (pages 60–63)
CONNECT & DISCUSS	Connect with one or two group members Discuss the follow-up questions (page 64)
CATCH UP & READ AHEAD (BEFORE WEEK 4 GROUP MEETING)	Read chapters 9–11 in *Every Thought Captive* Complete any unfinished studies (page 65)

THE PATTERN OF OFFENSE

[AND PLEASURE AND DESPAIR]

"In your anger do not sin": Do not let the sun go down while you are still angry, and do not give the devil a foothold. . . . And do not grieve the Holy Spirit of God, with whom you were sealed for the day of redemption. Get rid of all bitterness, rage and anger, brawling and slander, along with every form of malice. Be kind and compassionate to one another.

EPHESIANS 4:26–27, 30–32

WELCOME | READ ON YOUR OWN

Step onto any sailing vessel and you'll see crews mastering their craft—learning when to raise the sails, when to reef them, and when to change course. But perhaps the most important skill they develop isn't about handling the rigging—it's about reading the winds. Before any journey can succeed, a sailor must learn to pause, assess, and navigate with wisdom rather than reaction.

In our lives, we find ourselves on a different kind of sea. The world seems full of storms, with every social media post, comment, or unanswered text feeling like a potential wave threatening our stability. We move through life with our storm sails ready, treating every interaction like approaching weather. Like sailors studying the horizon, we scan every word and gesture for signs of brewing trouble.

Jesus, facing the ultimate tempest—betrayal, mockery, and crucifixion—demonstrated a response that defied natural instinct. Instead of battening down the hatches, he remained open. Instead of seeking safe harbor, he offered shelter to others. He showed us that true strength isn't found in how quickly we can turn away from rough waters but in how steadily we can extend peace amid the storm.

The pattern of offense can feel like a whirlpool dragging down our spirit, pulling us away from our ability to love, forgive, and grow. Yet just as sailors learn to navigate treacherous waters, so God offers us a way to break free from destructive currents. The key isn't in avoiding rough seas but in learning to pause, understand, and respond with grace. This spiritual discipline requires daily practice, just as sailors hone their skills through countless voyages.

CONNECT | 10 MINUTES

Get this session started by choosing one or both of the following questions to discuss together as a group:

- What is something that resonated with you in last week's personal study that you would like to share with the group?

- What are the biggest triggers for you when it comes to getting angry?

WATCH | 25 MINUTES

Now watch the video for this session. Below is an outline of the key points covered during the teaching. Record any important concepts that stand out to you.

OUTLINE

I. In today's world, we struggle more than ever with the pattern of offense.
   A. Social media has become a way to keep a daily inventory of who has offended us.
   B. Everyone today seems ready to take offense at the smallest thing.[26]
   C. The real battle when it comes to this pattern is what is taking place in our minds.

II. We need to understand the pattern of offense.
   A. Offense can feel good. It triggers a release of chemicals in our brains and gives us a sense of identity—even community—with others who have been offended.[27]
   B. Offense has a snowballing effect and can turn into an avalanche of anger.
   C. Taking offense can lead to anger, which easily leads to sin (Ephesians 4:26).
   D. As followers of Christ, we are to get rid of *all* bitterness, rage, anger, and *every* form of malice (Ephesians 4:31).

III. The Bible instructs us to *stop* before reacting when we feel offended.
   A. "Everyone should be quick to listen, slow to speak and slow to become angry, because human anger does not produce the righteousness that God desires" (James 1:19–20).
   B. Every time we make the decision to stop before just reacting, we learn a new pattern of responding to offense.

IV. Two important questions to ask ourselves when we feel offended:
   A. *Where is this coming from?* We need to stop when we feel offended and think of what might be below the surface that is causing it.
   B. *What would it be like?* When we seek to know the person who is offending us and his or her story, it allows us to respond with compassion (John 4:1–26).

V. We are to forgive one another as Christ forgave us (Ephesians 4:32).
   A. This allows us to replace the pattern of offense with a new pattern: *kindness*.
   B. We can choose to pray for those who have offended us rather than rehearse the offense in our minds.
   C. This is not about pretending that we are not hurt but choosing a different way in how we will respond.

NOTES

DISCUSS | 35 MINUTES

Discuss what you just watched by answering the following questions.

1. Today, it can seem as if people are walking around with their guard up and fist raised, just waiting to take a swing at the first person who offends them. Think about the last time you really felt offended. What was your immediate reaction? Looking back now, what underlying fears or insecurities might have been beneath the surface?

2. Surprisingly, being offended can trigger the release of dopamine in our brains—the "feel-good" chemical—when we experience something pleasurable. This is likely due to anticipation of social reward when we share our offense with others and get their validation. When is a time that you found this to be true? How do you think this release of dopamine in our brains reinforces and perpetuates the pattern of offense?

3. Ask someone to read aloud Ephesians 4:26–27. What practical wisdom do these verses offer for handling offense? How might anger give the devil a foothold in a person's life?

4. The Bible instructs us to *stop* before we respond to an offense. We pause when we feel offended and ask two important questions: "Where is this anger coming from?" and "What would it be like to be the other person?" Think of a recent time when you reacted in anger because of an offense. How might this approach have changed the outcome?

5. Ask someone to read aloud Colossians 3:12–14. What does this passage instruct us to remember before we lash out against someone who has offended us? When you look at Paul's words, what does it look like for you to "forgive as the Lord forgave you"?

RESPOND | 10 MINUTES

It is not natural for us to react with kindness, compassion, and forgiveness when someone offends us. It takes the power of the *Holy Spirit* and some retraining of our responses to live above the pattern of offense. Take a few minutes on your own to read the following instructions from James on how to jump-start this re-training process, and then answer the questions that follow.

> My dear brothers and sisters, take note of this: Everyone should be quick to listen, slow to speak and slow to become angry, because human anger does not produce the righteousness that God desires. Therefore, get rid of all moral filth and the evil that is so prevalent and humbly accept the word planted in you, which can save you.
>
> **JAMES 1:19–21**

How would the practice of being "quick to listen" change the way you experience and express anger? Share a specific example from your own relationships.

How would the practice of being "slow to speak" change the outcome of those times you feel offended? Share a specific example from your own relationships.

How can having the Word of God "planted" within you help you to respond with kindness, compassion, and forgiveness when you encounter offensive people?

PRAY | 10 MINUTES

Pray about breaking free from the pattern of offense. Be honest about your struggles and ask for God's help in developing new response patterns. Pray for wisdom to see beneath the surface of offensive situations and for grace to respond well. Before closing, write down prayer requests from the group related to handling offense.

SESSION THREE

PERSONAL STUDY

In the previous session, you examined some of the ways the world tries to shape you into its mold through the pattern of distraction and the pattern of insecurity. In this personal study, you will explore the pattern of offense that you discussed during this week's group time in more detail. You will also look at two other insidious patterns from the enemy that are especially prevalent in the world today: the pattern of pleasure and the pattern of despair. As always, be sure to record your responses to the questions, as you will be given a few minutes to share your insights and key takeaways at the start of the next session. If you are reading *Every Thought Captive* alongside this study, first review chapters 6–8 in the book.

THE SACRED PAUSE

In photography, one of the crucial skills is about finding the right distance. Before capturing any image, photographers must resist the urge to snap immediately. They practice stepping back, adjusting their perspective, and choosing their frame with deliberate care. This intentional distance between seeing and shooting often makes the difference between an ordinary snapshot and a powerful image.

The same principle applies in our battle against the pattern of offense. In our hyper-connected world, we face daily triggers—a passive-aggressive comment in a chat, a hostile social media post, a family member who knows how to provoke us. Our natural instinct, like an amateur photographer's impulse, is to react immediately to what we see, sharing our outrage before we've processed the moment. But wisdom calls us to adjust our focus—to pause so we can get a "sacred perspective."

This perspective shift isn't passive; it's an active choice that requires both courage and discipline. In 2 Samuel 16:5–12, we read how King David was cursed and insulted by a man named Shimei. David's mighty men—their warrior instincts demanding swift retribution—wanted to zoom in on the immediate conflict. But David chose to step back and consider whether God might be using this offense to compose a greater picture. Jesus also demonstrated the power of strategic restraint when he was insulted by the Sanhedrin (see Matthew 26:57–68). Not every provocative moment needs to be captured in our response.

Creating this sacred perspective takes practice. Just as photographers must train their eye to see beyond the obvious shot, we need to train ourselves to step back, refocus, and choose our response. We must learn to ask: *What is outside my current frame? What filters of past hurt might be coloring my view? How might my response affect the larger story God is telling through my life?*

Through consistent practice, what begins as a conscious effort can become a spiritual instinct—replacing our impulse for immediate reaction and retaliation with an eye for grace. Like a skilled photographer, we can learn to pause, adjust our spiritual lens, and respond with wisdom rather than reaction. We *can* create moments of redemption rather than conflict.

1. Start off by doing an assessment of how you typically respond when you feel offended. How would you rate how quickly you respond in these situations?

In person:

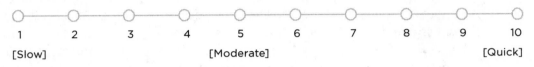

1	2	3	4	5	6	7	8	9	10
[Slow]				[Moderate]					[Quick]

Through text/email:

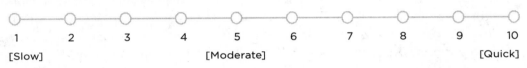

1	2	3	4	5	6	7	8	9	10
[Slow]				[Moderate]					[Quick]

On social media:

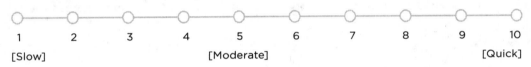

1	2	3	4	5	6	7	8	9	10
[Slow]				[Moderate]					[Quick]

2. Read Proverbs 12:16, 15:1, and 29:8. What guidance is given in these verses about a "gentle answer"? How would your relationships look different if you lived out these verses?

In Matthew 18:15, Jesus addresses how to respond when someone says or does something hurtful or offensive: "If another believer sins against you, go privately and point out the offense. If the other person listens and confesses it, you have won that person back" (NLT). Jesus says in cases of offense against us, we should go to the other person at once. We should be clear and specific about what offended us. In general, we should do it privately and with a spirit that desires reconciliation.[28] Can I just point out what Jesus *doesn't* say to do if someone offends us? (1) Immediately post a vague, passive-aggressive comment on social media. (2) Tell lots of people about it and call it a "prayer chain." (3) Find a Bible version that translates "turn the other cheek" as "roll your eyes." (4) Rehearse witty comebacks in the shower for the next three weeks. When an offense takes root, it grows into various weeds in our garden that can be difficult to pull up.[29]

3. Read Matthew 18:15–17. What would it look like if you consistently handled those who offended you in the way that Jesus advises in this passage?

4. Read Psalm 4:4 and 139:23–24. How might regular self-examination and asking God to "search" your heart help you develop better responses to offense? List three specific ways.

1.	
2.	
3.	

To help us capture angry thoughts and replace them with thoughts that are obedient to Christ, I want to give us one word to remember when we start losing our temporal lobe. The word is *stop*. If you're a "picture is worth a thousand words" kind of person, you might imagine a stop sign. When you start to feel angry, think of the word *stop*, or picture in your head the image of a stop sign. This strategy is rooted in Scripture. It's a way to apply our key verse—to take our runaway, self-destructive, harmful thoughts captive. And it's also confirmed by modern research. If you were to go to an anger management course, one technique they teach is called "thought stopping."[30]

5. Today, practice taking your thoughts captive by using the "3-3-3 Technique." When you feel offended, take 3 deep breaths; then come up with 3 possible reasons for the other person's behavior; and then consider 3 different ways you could respond. After giving this a try, write down how this practice could help you respond to offense in a more godly way.

How this could help you respond to offense in a more godly way:

FROM CRAVING TO CONTENTMENT

We are under assault. Each day, we are confronted with anywhere between four thousand to ten thousand advertisements and messages in the media—most promising happiness through instant gratification.[31] This relentless exposure not only impacts our purchasing habits but also rewires our brains, programming discontent as our default state. Our hearts, designed to find profound joy in God, have become ensnared in an endless cycle. We dart restlessly from one fleeting pleasure to the next, always searching for peace but never finding it.

In Ecclesiastes, we read of how King Solomon went on the ultimate shopping spree of life—trying out everything his money, power, and privilege could buy. But in the end, he came to a realization: "Meaningless! Meaningless! . . . Everything is meaningless!" (Ecclesiastes 12:8). Everything the world offered left him feeling *empty*.

Sound familiar? It's like when we convince ourselves the next promotion, or relationship, or vacation will finally make us happy. Somehow, we end up where Solomon did—holding all the things that promised to fill us up but just left us wanting more.

In our age of instant gratification, we face a decision: Will we allow our minds to be molded by the world's pleasure paradigm? Or will we cultivate our capacity to find satisfaction in Christ alone? The answer requires more than just passive resistance. It demands active engagement in reshaping our desires and expectations.

Every day presents us with countless small decisions that either strengthen our relationship with God or pull us toward the world's empty promises. Each choice we make either reinforces the world's narrative of instant gratification or builds our capacity to find lasting fulfillment in God's presence.

The path forward isn't about denying our desires but about redirecting them toward their intended purpose. When we recognize our longing for satisfaction is actually a God-given hunger for something greater than what this world offers, we can begin to see even our discontent as an invitation to deeper relationship with him.

1. Read Ecclesiastes 12:13–14. Solomon has just stated—referring to the pleasures of this world—that "everything is meaningless" (verse 8). What conclusion does he reach in these verses as to what *does* have meaning? What does this say about the pattern of pleasure?

2. Look up Proverbs 21:17, 21. Where does the path lead for those who pursue pleasure? Where does the path lead for those who pursue righteousness?

We're all in danger of getting caught up and trapped in the world's pleasure pattern. We need to understand the progression of thoughts because if we don't take these thoughts captive, it's only a matter of time before they take us captive. This progression is: (1) *Doing what feels good will make me happy*; (2) *I deserve to be happy, right now*; (3) *Pleasure is determined by my immediate circumstances*; and (4) *I'll have pleasure when I get what I don't have.*[32]

3. Think about the pattern of pleasure and this progression in your life. How often would you say you find yourself thinking the following thoughts?

I believe doing what feels good will make me happy:

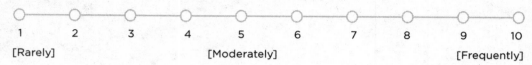

1	2	3	4	5	6	7	8	9	10
[Rarely]				[Moderately]				[Frequently]	

I believe that I deserve to be happy, right now:

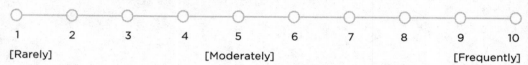

1	2	3	4	5	6	7	8	9	10
[Rarely]				[Moderately]				[Frequently]	

I believe my happiness is determined by my immediate circumstances:

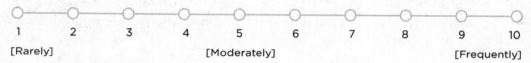

1	2	3	4	5	6	7	8	9	10
[Rarely]				[Moderately]				[Frequently]	

I believe I will be happy when I get what I don't have.

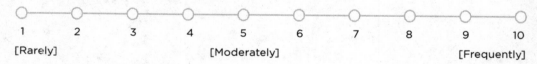

1	2	3	4	5	6	7	8	9	10
[Rarely]				[Moderately]				[Frequently]	

We think pleasure is found in getting what we don't have or getting what *they've* got. We're usually thinking not about what we already have, but rather about what we want. Instead, the Bible teaches us to take pleasure in what we already have. First Thessalonians 5:16–18 reads, "Rejoice always, pray continually, give thanks in all circumstances." We're not told to be thankful *for* all circumstances, but we can be thankful *in* all circumstances. Intentional thankfulness and gratitude shape our brains so that we stop noticing what is missing and start being more aware of what we have been given. Choosing gratitude is how we take unhappy thoughts captive.[33]

4. Consider Paul's words in 1 Thessalonians 5:16–18. How might practicing gratitude challenge your current thoughts about happiness? What holds you back from being more thankful?

5. Read Philippians 4:11–13. Paul states in this passage that he learned to be content in any circumstance by finding his satisfaction in Christ. Consider your typical daily routine. Using the table below, identify specific moments when you are most vulnerable to pleasure-seeking and what you could focus on instead.

Time of day	Common pleasure trigger	Alternate focus
Morning		
Midday		
Evening		
Before bed		

STUDY 3

SPIRALING THOUGHTS

The statistics are alarming. Since 1999, there has been a dramatic increase in "deaths by despair," defined as deaths by suicide, drug and alcohol poisoning, and alcoholic liver disease and cirrhosis.[34] As one researcher noted, "Mortality from deaths of despair far surpasses anything seen in America since the dawn of the twentieth century." [35] Another report states, "Deaths from these three conditions have risen so much that they have been cited as a major contributor to the recent decline in the overall life expectancy in the United States."[36]

This isn't just a troubling trend but also something that reveals a fundamental truth about our minds: Our thought patterns can either trap us in despair or lead us toward hope. It begins with *distorted thinking*—viewing a situation in an inaccurate way that puts it in a negative light. This become *discouragement*—dwelling on the negative thoughts without seeking a solution. This leads to *disillusionment*—a loss in faith that things will ever get better. Finally, it turns into *despair*—a conclusion that there is no way out.

This struggle isn't unique to our anxious age. Even the most powerful and effective servants of God grappled with the pull of despair. In 1 Kings 19:1–9, we read how Elijah, after his triumph against the prophets of Baal at Mount Carmel, became so overwhelmed by fear that he fled into the wilderness. Once there, he prayed, "I have had enough, LORD . . . take my life" (verse 4). What makes Elijah's story particularly relevant is that God's response wasn't to criticize his feelings or dismiss them. Instead, he invited Elijah to bring his anxiety to him.

In today's environment of constant stress and negative news, we can either allow our negative thoughts to overwhelm us or learn to go to God with our struggles. Like Elijah, we're not necessarily wrestling with irrational fears—often our troubles are very real. The challenge isn't to eliminate all the problems from our lives but to consciously choose to talk to God about our despair *and* talk to our despair about God. This simple shift in focus can make all the difference between drowning in our thoughts and finding solid ground in his presence.

1. In a typical week, how often do you find yourself struggling with the following?

Ruminating on past mistakes or future worries:

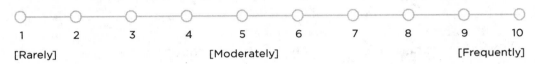

1   2   3   4   5   6   7   8   9   10

[Rarely]   [Moderately]   [Frequently]

Trying to handle overwhelming feelings by yourself:

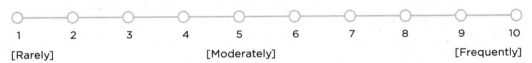

1   2   3   4   5   6   7   8   9   10

[Rarely]   [Moderately]   [Frequently]

Starting your day focused on anxious thoughts:

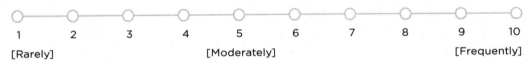

1   2   3   4   5   6   7   8   9   10

[Rarely]   [Moderately]   [Frequently]

2. Read Psalm 55:1–5. David begins this psalm with a plea for God's help. As he continues to pray, he gets specific about what is stressing him out and causing his despair—his enemies. Think about something that is causing you anxiety right now. Write out a prayer below in which you turn that general anxiety into a specific prayer to God for help.

David starts off being honest with God about his despair. Then—and this is huge—he begins to be honest with himself about who God is. He stops talking to God about his despair and starts talking to his despair about God. David reminds himself who God is, what God has done, and what God will do. . . . The way we overcome negative thinking, strongholds, and the world's mold is to capture our thoughts and make them obedient to Christ. That's what David does here. He captures his despairing thoughts and renews his mind by telling himself truths about God. It's what we need to learn to do as well.[37]

3. Read Psalm 55:6–19. David begins this section of his psalm by expressing what he would like to do in the moment—"fly away and be at rest." But he then reminds himself of God's nature. What are a few of the truths that David tells himself about the Lord?

4. David *consistently* cried out to God—"evening, morning and noon" (verse 17). What practical steps could you take today to establish a similar rhythm of connecting with God? Be specific about when, where, and how you could do this.

When:

Where:

How:

David begins in a state of distress because he has enemies lining up against him. He is overwhelmed. But he prays honestly and specifically. He asks God to jump into the driver's seat. Morning, noon, and night, he reminds himself who God is and what God has done. David isn't worried anymore; he is worshiping. As he prays, he is reminded of who God is, and he can't help but praise God. As he does, his worship drowns out his worry. I'm not sure worship and worry can coexist. It doesn't mean the problems go away, that the anxiety goes away. But it loses much of its power over us. The pattern of desperation gives way to the pattern of dependence.[38]

5. Read Psalm 55:22–23. What conclusion did David reach by the end of his psalm? What did he acknowledge about God when it came to his worries?

CONNECT AND DISCUSS

Take time today to connect with a group member and talk about some of the insights from this session. Use any of the prompts below to help guide your discussion.

Which elements of this session about patterns of offense, pleasure, and despair caught your attention the most? Why those particular elements?

What are some of the ways the pattern of offense manifests in your life?

What are some of the ways the world promotes the pattern of pleasure?

What helps you to recognize and fight against the pattern of despair?

How do you see the patterns of offense, pleasure, and despair negatively impacting your relationships with people and your relationship with God?

CATCH UP AND READ AHEAD

Use this time to go back and complete any of the study and reflection questions from previous days that you weren't able to finish. Make a note below of any revelations you've had and reflect on any growth or personal insights you've gained.

Read chapters 9–11 in *Every Thought Captive* before the next group session. Use the space below to make note of anything in those chapters that inspires you, stands out to you, or encourages you.

WEEK 4

BEFORE GROUP MEETING	Read chapters 9–11 in *Every Thought Captive* Read the Welcome section (page 68)
GROUP MEETING	Discuss the Connect questions Watch the video teaching for session 4 Discuss the questions that follow as a group Do the closing exercise and pray (pages 68–72)
STUDY 1	Complete the personal study (pages 74–77)
STUDY 2	Complete the personal study (pages 78–81)
STUDY 3	Complete the personal study (pages 82–85)
CONNECT & DISCUSS	Connect with one or two group members Discuss the follow-up questions (page 86)
CATCH UP & READ AHEAD (BEFORE WEEK 5 GROUP MEETING)	Read chapters 12–13 in *Every Thought Captive* Complete any unfinished studies (page 87)

SESSION FOUR

SAY IT OUT LOUD

The words of the mouth are deep waters, but the fountain of wisdom is a rushing stream. . . . From the fruit of their mouth a person's stomach is filled; with the harvest of their lips they are satisfied. The tongue has the power of life and death, and those who love it will eat its fruit.

PROVERBS 18:4, 20–21

WELCOME | READ ON YOUR OWN

Stand by a flowing river and you'll notice something remarkable: Every current and ripple shapes the course of the water's journey. Nothing moves without influence—from the gentlest eddy to the strongest surge, each movement affects what follows. Our minds work in much the same way. They constantly flow with the words we speak to ourselves, creating patterns that shape our lives in profound ways.

We all carry internal rivers of thought that flow through the channels of our minds. Sometimes these waters run turbulent with words spoken years ago—a teacher's harsh criticism, a parent's moment of frustration, a friend's painful betrayal. Like water carving through stone, these words have created deep channels in our minds, shaping how we see ourselves and the world around us. They become the underlying current of our daily lives, influencing our decisions and relationships.

But here's the transformative truth that can change everything: Just as God spoke light into darkness at creation, so he has given us power to speak *new life* over our circumstances. This occurs not through empty self-help mantras or positive thinking but by declaring the eternal truth of God that transcends our temporary struggles. "Gracious words are a honeycomb, sweet to the soul and healing to the bones" (Proverbs 16:24). Proclaiming God's words has the power to bring about *healing*.

Speaking words is the tool God has chosen to bring power into the world. So the choice lies before us. Will we to allow the turbulent waters of defeat and erode our path? Or will we choose a new course by beginning to speak words of life that align with God's truth about who we are and who we are called to be?

CONNECT | 10 MINUTES

Get this session started by choosing one or both of the following questions to discuss together as a group:

- What is something that resonated with you in last week's personal study that you would like to share with the group?

- What is one of the most common things you heard from a parent (or an-other influential person) growing up? What made it so memorable?

WATCH | 25 MINUTES

Now watch the video for this session. Below is an outline of the key points covered during the teaching. Record any key concepts that stand out to you.

OUTLINE

I. The words we speak to ourselves have power in shaping our lives.

   A. In a vision, God instructed the prophet Ezekiel to *speak* his word over the dry bones to restore them back to life (Ezekiel 37:1–6).

   B. When God created the world, he spoke it into existence (Genesis 1:1–27).

   C. Jesus brought the dead back to life by speaking words (Luke 7:14; John 11:43).

II. The words we speak program our subconscious minds.

   A. Words aren't just expressions of thoughts—they create and reinforce thoughts.

   B. Every time we speak, the words we voice become a thought.

III. Science reveals that words have the power of life and death (Proverbs 18:21).

   A. The words we speak direct the part of our brain called the *reticular activating system*, which gives attention to information confirming or aligning with our verbal assertions.[39]

   B. Our words train our brains what to look for, what to pay attention to, and what is important.

   C. When we speak words, our brains release neurotransmitters that help us feel better[40] and strengthen our immune system.[41]

IV. We can rewire our brains by speaking God's life-giving truths to ourselves.

   A. The power comes in speaking *God's* words over our lives.

   B. God's words are like seeds planted in our minds—and they always bear fruit (Isaiah 55:10–11).

   C. Patience is required in this process, but we can be assured that when we plant the seed of God's truth and cultivate it, that seed will grow and bear fruit.

V. Rewiring our minds to believe God's truth begins by noticing the "recordings" playing in our minds.

   A. The first step is to notice what words we are actually saying to ourselves.

   B. We then run those thoughts through the filter of Philippians 4:8—"whatever is true, whatever is noble, whatever is right, whatever is pure, whatever is lovely, whatever is admirable."

   C. We then speak other words of God to ourselves that are found in Scripture. As we say these truths out loud, we break down enemy strongholds.

NOTES

_____
_____
_____
_____
_____
_____
_____
_____
_____
_____
_____
_____
_____
_____
_____
_____
_____
_____
_____
_____
_____
_____
_____
_____
_____
_____
_____
_____
_____
_____
_____
_____

DISCUSS | 35 MINUTES

Discuss what you just watched by answering the following questions.

1. Think about the "recording" that plays the most in your mind. What messages do you hear repeatedly? Where do you think these messages originated?

2. Ask someone to read aloud Ezekiel 37:1–6. What strikes you about God's instruction for Ezekiel to speak to the dry bones in the valley? How might this relate to speaking life into "dead" areas of your own life?

3. Speaking words *out loud* engages multiple regions of the brain, including the frontal lobe, the temporal lobe, the parietal lobe, and the motor cortex. Speaking something out loud can actually help make it stick in your memory! How would you describe the difference (in terms of impact) between just *thinking* something and *declaring* it out loud?

4. Ask someone to read aloud Proverbs 12:18 and 18:21. When is a time in your life that someone's words pierced like a sword and brought about death—whether that was the death of a dream, the death a relationship, or the death of something else? When is a time that someone's words brought healing and life to your situation?

5. Now ask someone to read aloud Philippians 4:8. Remember, this is the filter through which you should run your words and thoughts to make sure they measure up with God's truth. What are some words that you say to yourself that you know do not measure up when run through this filter? What needs to change in your thinking regarding these messages?

RESPOND | 10 MINUTES

God's words are like seeds that bear good fruit. However, we have to plant those seeds in the "soil" of our minds if we want to see a harvest. Take a few minutes on your own to read God's words about this in the following passage, and then answer the questions that follow.

> As the rain and the snow come down from heaven, and do not return to it without watering the earth and making it bud and flourish, so that it yields seed for the sower and bread for the eater, so is my word that goes out from my mouth: It will not return to me empty, but will accomplish what I desire and achieve the purpose for which I sent it.
>
> ISAIAH 55:10-11

What imagery does God use in this passage to describe how his word comes to you?

God states that his word will "not return to me empty." Think of a time when a passage or verse of Scripture impacted your life in an unexpected way. How did it change you?

What "dry ground" in your life right now needs the water of God's Word spoken over it?

PRAY | 10 MINUTES

As a group, pray about the words that you speak to yourselves and to others. Be honest about the negative recordings that play in your mind and ask for God's help in replacing them with his truth. Pray for the courage to speak God's truth and life into dead places. Before closing, write down any specific prayer requests from the group related to the power of words.

PERSONAL STUDY

Have you ever considered the recording that plays in your mind each day—the words you speak to yourself when you wake up, look in the mirror, face challenges, or lie down at night? In this week's personal study, you will explore passages from Scripture that will continue to help you examine the words you speak to yourself, discover how they align with God's truth, and learn how to replace harmful thoughts with life-giving declarations from God's Word. As you work through these exercises, keep writing down your responses to the questions, as you will be given a few minutes to share your insights at the start of the next session. If you are reading *Every Thought Captive* alongside this study, first review chapters 9–11 in the book.

REPLACING THE SOUNDTRACK

Have you ever had an "earworm"? The chances are likely you have if you live in the Western world, as researchers say that up to 98 percent of people have had them.[42] We are not talking here about any type of soil-dwelling invertebrate that has somehow lodged itself in your ear. Rather, *earworm* is a technical term that describes an unwanted catchy tune that repeats in your head.

What is interesting is that this same phenomenon happens with the soundtrack that plays in your mind. Every life has one—the constant narrative that plays in the back of your mind. This internal dialogue shapes your reality more powerfully than any external voice. Like a movie score that colors how you interpret each scene, these internal words influence how you experience every moment of your life, from your greatest triumph to your deepest struggle. And, just like an earworm, certain phrases can get stuck on repeat in your brain.

Think about the last time you looked in the mirror. What words played in your mind? Or the last time you faced a challenge. What narrative accompanied that moment? Or the last time you endured a setback. What internal voice did you hear in that instance? Most likely, you heard a familiar soundtrack that was recorded years ago. Maybe you picked up this "earworm" back in school when someone said, "You will never amount to anything." Or perhaps you acquired it in a home where words of criticism outweighed words of grace. Like deeply worn grooves in vinyl, those messages created patterns in your thinking that now play automatically, shaping your self-image and limiting your potential without you even realizing it.

So how do you get rid of an earworm? One technique is to seek out the tune in question, as earworms often occur when you remember only part of a song.[43] Another technique is to replace the annoying song with a different tune.[44] These same techniques work when it comes to replacing the words you say to yourself. By seeking out the *source* of your internal dialogue, you can uncover where those negative words were spoken to you and recognize that they no longer have power over you. You can then *replace* those destructive thoughts—those lies from the enemy—by listening to the "song" that God has for your life.

1. It's time to check what earworms you have when it comes to the soundtrack that plays in your mind. What messages do you most frequently hear in the following areas?

Messages about your worth:

Messages about your capabilities:

Messages about your future:

God's words are like seeds that get planted, seeds that always bear fruit. And that's what we want to do—start planting the seeds of God's words in our minds and in our lives. Maybe you've been planting some seeds of God's Word and the fruit doesn't come right away. You feel like the planting isn't making any difference. I understand the frustration, but you need to remember that this is the way seeds typically work. Farmers plant the seed, and then . . . they wait. Patience is required because fruit is coming.[45]

2. Read Galatians 6:7–10. What two types of "seeds" can you sow in your mind? Which category do the internal messages that you just identified fall into?

3. One of the techniques to get rid of an earworm is to seek out the song that is replaying in your mind. Do the same with the internal messages you identified.

Internal message	Where did this message come from?
Worth:	
Capabilities:	
Future:	

Jesus warned us about words carelessly spoken in Matthew 12:36–37: "Let me tell you something: Every one of these careless words is going to come back to haunt you. There will be a time of Reckoning. Words are powerful; take them seriously. Words can be your salvation. Words can also be your damnation" (MSG). Jesus took very seriously the words we speak, including those we speak not so seriously. He warns us that even our careless words *have the power of life and death*. We need to pay attention to the careless words we speak to others, but also to the careless words we speak to ourselves. It's so easy for the words that have wounded us to become the soundtrack of our lives.[46]

4. A second technique to get rid of an earworm is to replace it with a different song. You can do this with the negative messages that play in your mind by choosing to replace them with positive messages based on God's Word. Do this now by looking up the following passages and writing down how they counter the negative messages you say to yourself.

Negative message	God's truth about you
I am inadequate . . .	2 Corinthians 3:5–6:
I can't overcome this challenge . . .	Philippians 4:13:
I am worthless . . .	1 Peter 2:9:
I have no future . . .	Jeremiah 29:11:

5. The psalmist wrote, "Sing to the LORD a new song; sing to the LORD, all the earth" (Psalm 96:1). What is the "new song" that you feel God is calling you to sing about yourself?

CALLING LIFE FROM DEATH

Stand with Ezekiel for a moment in that valley of dry bones. Feel the crunch beneath your feet. See the lifeless remains scattered as far as the eye can reach—a graveyard stretched across the horizon. The air itself seems heavy with the weight of death and ending. In this desolate place, God asks a seemingly absurd question: "Can these bones live?" It's a question that echoes through time into our own valleys of death and disappointment.

We all have such valleys. Perhaps it's a marriage that feels devoid of love—a skeleton of what it once was—where even simple conversations feel like walking through a graveyard of hurts. Maybe it's a dream that lies scattered and broken, like bones bleached by years of disappointments. It could be a relationship with a child that feels beyond repair, where every interaction only seems to confirm the death of what once was filled with life. A career might feel like a graveyard of missed opportunities. Faith can become dry and brittle from seasons of doubt and unanswered prayers. "Can these bones live?"

Notice God's instructions to Ezekiel in that valley. He doesn't tell him to perform CPR on the bones. He doesn't instruct Ezekiel to arrange them properly or to wish really hard for life to return. He doesn't even tell him to pray about it. Instead, God commands him to speak—to prophesy to these dry bones. Ezekiel is to declare life where there is only death, proclaim hope where there is only despair, and voice victory where there is only defeat.

This isn't just a dramatic Old Testament moment; it is a pattern God established from creation itself. God spoke light into darkness, order into chaos, life into the void. Jesus spoke to storms and they obeyed, to diseases and they fled, to death and it retreated. Our words, when aligned with God's truth, carry the same life-giving power. They become carriers of his creative force and conduits of his resurrection power.

Paul wrote, "The Spirit of God, who raised Jesus from the dead, lives in you" (Romans 8:11 NLT). The *same power* that raised Christ from the dead can breathe new life into your dead places. Our part is to declare God's truth and not remain silent in our graveyards.

1. Take another look at Ezekiel 37:1–6, which you examined during this week's group time. What did God instruct Ezekiel to say over the bones? What promise did the Lord make?

2. Identify some of the "dry bones" in your life. What areas feel lifeless? What makes it difficult to believe God could bring new life to this situation?

Relationship dry bones:

Spiritual dry bones:

Personal dry bones:

God promises Ezekiel that he will put flesh and muscles and skin on the bones and breathe life into them, and he makes the same promise to us. But *how*? What did God tell Ezekiel to do to bring life to the dead bones? *Speak*. Not pray, not visualize, not touch, not work. He tells Ezekiel to speak. Just like a mom with a sobbing, stammering toddler, God tells Ezekiel, "Use your words." With those words, the dead "will come to life. Then you will know that I am the Lord" (Ezekiel 37:6 NLT).[47]

3. Notice that God commanded Ezekiel to speak to the bones, not just observe them. Where in your life might God be calling you to speak his truth into what appears lifeless?

4. "Words can bring death or life" (Proverbs 18:21 CEV). What words of death (negative words) have you been speaking over each of these situations?

Over your marriage/relationships:
Over your children/family:
Over your career:
Over your faith:

Ezekiel spoke, and it worked. The bones started rattling and coming together. Muscles and flesh and skin formed over the bones. It was working, but it wasn't enough. They still had "no breath in them." So now what? . . . God tells Ezekiel to speak again. Ezekiel listens to what God said. Then Ezekiel speaks what God said. Then Ezekiel watches what God does. Then Ezekiel listens again to what God said. Then Ezekiel speaks again what God said. Then Ezekiel watches again what God does. It's going to be the same for us.[48]

5. Read Ezekiel 37:7–10. Ezekiel had to prophesy twice—once to the bones and once to the breath. It's the same for you. You listen to what God says and then speak what God just said. Then you do it again . . . and again. And if you keep saying it out loud, God will do for you what he did in the valley of dry bones. Start this process today by declaring God's truths over the following situations—and then do it again and again throughout the week.

Over my relationships, I declare these words of life . . .

Over my children and family, I declare these words of life . . .

Over my career, I declare these words of life . . .

Over my faith, I declare these words of life . . .

WIELDING THE WEAPON

There is a difference between reading God's Word silently and declaring it over your life. When you speak Scripture out loud, something powerful happens—your ears hear what your mouth is saying and your brain processes those truth-filled words. It's like turning up the volume on God's truth while simultaneously turning down the volume on the lies that have played in your head.

It is no accident that the Bible is referred to as a *sword*. Paul instructs us to take up "the sword of the Spirit, which is the word of God" (Ephesians 6:17). Another author writes that the Bible is "sharper than any double-edged sword, it penetrates even to dividing soul and spirit, joints and marrow; it judges the thoughts and attitudes of the heart" (Hebrews 4:12). The Bible is a *weapon* in your hands—a powerful tool that you use to combat all those negative recordings in your life.

Jesus' temptation in the wilderness provides an example for how you should use the "sword of the Spirit." As you might recall, "Jesus was led by the Spirit into the wilderness to be tempted by the devil" (Matthew 4:1). There he fasted for forty days and forty nights and—of course—was hungry. The enemy saw this as an opportunity and came to Jesus with a temptation to turn stones to bread. Then the devil tempted Jesus to demonstrate his power by throwing himself down from the temple. Satan then tried to get Jesus to shortcut his mission by promising to give him the world.

How did Jesus respond to each of these temptations? By reciting, out loud, the Word of God. Jesus had memorized Scripture. He knew exactly which strike to make with his "sword" to counter each of the enemy's attacks. When you memorize Scripture and speak it out loud, you do the same. In doing so, remember that you are not just repeating religious words. You are actually wielding the *same power that God used to create the universe.*

Speaking God's Word aloud does something else—it builds your faith. As Paul writes, "Faith comes by hearing, and hearing by the word of God" (Romans 10:17 NKJV). When you speak Scripture aloud, you're actually increasing your faith. Each spoken word becomes a seed planted in the soil of your heart . . . destined to produce a harvest of God's truth in your life.

1. Read Luke 4:1–13. What does this story reveal about how Satan makes his attacks? How have you seen the enemy employ these same tactics in your life?

The phrase "take captive" in 2 Corinthians 10:5 comes from the Greek word *aichmalotizo*—a military term that means to capture an enemy combatant or to lead a prisoner away. Paul is using warfare imagery to describe our struggle against harmful thoughts. We are to treat our thoughts as if they were enemy soldiers in a spiritual battle. We are not to negotiate with them or let them roam free, but rather to decisively take them prisoner. Adopting this strategy empowers us to take an active role in our mental processes rather than being passive victims of our thoughts.[49]

2. The devil is described in Scripture as "a roaring lion looking for someone to devour" (1 Peter 5:8). What does this tell you about how you should deal with him? What is the danger of trying to "negotiate" or "reason" with a roaring lion?

3. Look up Psalm 34:10–14. What does this passage say you should do if you love life and want to "see many good days"? What does it mean to "keep your tongue from evil"?

In this battle of the mind, don't ever think, *I'm all alone.* You are not out there by yourself practicing the power of positive thinking. This isn't you sitting by yourself in an ice bath practicing mind control. . . . This is a team operation. You are taking your thoughts captive, but you're doing it with the help of the Holy Spirit. Jesus called the Holy Spirit our helper. One of the ways the Spirit helps us is by guiding our thoughts. . . . The Holy Spirit will bring supernatural awareness to your thoughts, help you remember Bible verses, and teach you how to apply them to your life.[50]

4. Read the words of Jesus to his disciples in John 14:25–27. Jesus promised to send the Holy Spirit, "the Advocate," to help them in the fight against the enemy. What did Jesus say the Holy Spirit would do? When have you witnessed the Holy Spirit do the same in your life?

5. Each time you speak God's Word *out loud,* it is reinforced in your life. You gradually begin to overcome the lies you have believed and replace them with God's life-giving truth. In this way, you increase your faith and trust in Christ. So, as you close out this week's personal study, think about when and where in your daily routine you can create designated "speaking spots" to proclaim the words of Scripture over your life.

In your morning routine:

At work or at school:

In the afternoon or on the commute home:

In the evening hours:

CONNECT AND DISCUSS

Take time today to connect with a group member and talk about some of the insights from this session. Use any of the prompts below to help guide your discussion.

Which elements of this session about speaking the truth of God's Word out loud especially resonated with you? Why those particular elements?

How would you summarize what the Bible says about the power of words?

What are some of the negative messages you found that echo in your mind?

What doubts do you have about your ability to rewire your brain and see positive change in your life through the power of repeating God's truth to yourself?

What are some verses you will memorize to combat the enemy's lies?

CATCH UP AND READ AHEAD

Use this time to go back and complete any of the study and reflection questions from previous days that you weren't able to finish. Make a note below of any revelations you've had and reflect on any growth or personal insights you've gained.

Read chapters 12–13 in *Every Thought Captive* before the next group session. Use the space below to make note of anything in those chapters that inspires you, stands out to you, or encourages you.

WEEK 5

BEFORE GROUP MEETING	Read chapters 12–13 in *Every Thought Captive* Read the Welcome section (page 90)
GROUP MEETING	Discuss the Connect questions Watch the video teaching for session 5 Discuss the questions that follow as a group Do the closing exercise and pray (pages 90–94)
STUDY 1	Complete the personal study (pages 96–99)
STUDY 2	Complete the personal study (pages 100–103)
STUDY 3	Complete the personal study (pages 104–107)
CONNECT & DISCUSS	Connect with one or two group members Discuss the follow-up questions (page 108)
WRAP IT UP	Complete any unfinished studies (page 109) Connect with your group about the next study that you want to go through together

WIN THE MORNING

Yet this I call to mind and therefore I have hope: Because of the Lord's great love we are not consumed, for his compassions never fail. They are new every morning; great is your faithfulness. I say to myself, "The Lord is my portion; therefore I will wait for him." The Lord is good to those whose hope is in him, to the one who seeks him.

LAMENTATIONS 3:21–25

WELCOME | READ ON YOUR OWN

Each morning before dawn, something sacred unfolds. The world holds its breath as darkness gives way to light, stillness yields to stirring, and a new day emerges with its untold possibilities. But in these precious moments, a battle is already beginning—a battle for our minds.

Our first thoughts in the morning set the trajectory of our day. If we fill our minds by immediately checking our phones, it sets us on a trajectory of distraction, stress, and edginess. (It's scientifically proven.[51]) But if we determine to take our thoughts captive and fill our minds with what is true, good, lovely, excellent, and praiseworthy, it sets us on a trajectory for transformation and the renewing of our minds. We are much less likely to be conformed to the patterns of the world as the day continues.

The heroes of our faith understood this truth. Abraham rose early to set out for a place of worship (see Genesis 22:3–5). Moses rose early to meet with God (see Exodus 24:4). Jesus himself sought solitude in the morning darkness (see Mark 1:35). They knew something we often forget: What we think in the waking moments has the power to shape everything that follows.

In a world that demands our immediate attention, we face a choice. Will we let the world set our mind's direction? Or will we align our thoughts with God's truth before the day unfolds? The battle for our minds isn't won in the heat of the day's challenges but in those quiet early moments when the sun first peeks over the horizon. Just as a garden must be tended before weeds take root, so our thoughts must be cultivated in the morning light, before the world attempts to plant its patterns in our minds.

CONNECT | 10 MINUTES

Get this session started by choosing one or both of the following questions to discuss together as a group:

- What is something that resonated with you in last week's personal study that you would like to share with the group?

- What is your favorite thing about mornings? Is there a part of your morning routine that you especially enjoy?

WATCH | 25 MINUTES

Now watch the video for this session. Below is an outline of the key points covered during the teaching. Record any key concepts that stand out to you.

OUTLINE

I. The thoughts we think in the morning have the power to determine the trajectory of our lives.
   A. How we start our day determines how we will handle everything that comes our way.
   B. Intentional morning routines can reduce stress, boost energy levels, and lower anxiety.
   C. Starting the day without engaging in critical spiritual preparation is much like jumping straight into running a marathon without first warming up.

II. The heroes of our faith maintained this consistent pattern of early morning intentionality.
   A. Abraham, Moses, Gideon, Hezekiah, and Job all rose early to meet with God.
   B. David often wrote of seeking God in the mornings (Psalm 5:3; 143:8; 59:16; 88:13).
   C. Jesus rose early in the morning to go to a solitary place to pray (Mark 1:35).

III. Our mornings—whenever they start—are the most important parts of our day.
   A. When we start our morning with intention, we bring those wins into the rest of the day.
   B. While we cannot control everything that happens to us during the day, we can control how we will prepare our minds to respond to those events.

IV. Winning the morning is like compound interest for our souls.
   A. Our consistent investments with God will add up over time.
   B. God gives us a fresh start every morning—a new beginning (Lamentations 3:22–23).
   C. Transformation happens one morning at time, one thought at a time, one choice at a time.

V. There are a few questions we need to consider regarding our morning routines.
   A. What voices have access to our minds first thing in the morning?
   B. What is the biggest obstacle keeping us from establishing a meaningful morning routine?
   C. Where could we create space in our home to invite reflection and spiritual connection?

NOTES

DISCUSS | 35 MINUTES

Discuss what you just watched by answering the following questions.

1. Think about your typical morning routine. What are usually your first thoughts or actions of the day? How do you see them affecting the rest of your day?

2. Ask someone to read aloud Mark 1:35. What strikes you about Jesus' morning priorities? What does this tell you about the importance of how you start your day?

3. A study published in the *Harvard Business Review* found that 92 percent of highly productive people follow planned morning routines.[52] What barriers keep you from establishing a consistent morning routine? How might you overcome those barriers?

4. Ask someone to read aloud Lamentations 3:22–23. The author writes that God's mercies are "new every morning." How might this truth impact how you approach each day? How could actively looking for God's new mercies change your morning mindset?

5. Morning routines are like compound interest for your soul. Even a small investment in spending time with God each morning will accumulate and yield rewards over time. In what ways have you seen the small yet consistent morning habits you are making (either positive or negative) compound over time in your life?

RESPOND | 10 MINUTES

David is described in the Bible as "a man after [God's] own heart" (1 Samuel 13:14). As we discover in the Psalms, he had a habit of focusing on God early in the morning. He knew God was always ready to hear from him, so he woke up ready to talk to him. Take a few minutes on your own to read the following verses, and then answer the questions that follow.

> In the morning, LORD, you hear my voice; in the morning I lay my requests before you and wait expectantly.

PSALM 5:3

> Let the morning bring me word of your unfailing love, for I have put my trust in you. Show me the way I should go, for to you I entrust my life.

PSALM 143:8

What specific elements of a morning routine do you see in these verses?

What would your ideal God-centered morning routine look like?

What one change could you make to move closer to "winning your morning"?

PRAY | 10 MINUTES

As a group, pray about your morning routines and habits. Be honest about the challenges you face in the morning hours and ask for God's help in establishing new patterns. Pray for discipline and commitment to guard these important morning moments. Before closing, write down specific prayer requests from the group related to morning routines and habits.

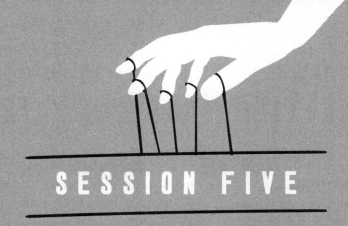

SESSION FIVE

PERSONAL STUDY

In this study, you have been exploring how to take every thought captive. In this week's group time, you discussed one final practice that can help you do this: *winning your mornings*. Just as Jesus sought solitude in the early hours to commune with his heavenly Father, so you have the same opportunity to set the spiritual trajectory of your day in those first precious moments. The thoughts you think—and the choices you make—in the morning hours can either anchor you in God's truth or leave you adrift in the world's chaos. As you work through these daily exercises, continue to journal your responses, reflections, and breakthroughs. If you are reading *Every Thought Captive* alongside this study, first read chapters 12–13 in the book.

SETTING YOUR DAILY TRAJECTORY

Each morning comes with a crucial decision point. Those first conscious moments determine the shape of everything that follows. The world knows this. This is why your phone lights up with notifications the moment you wake, with emails demanding immediate response and social media algorithms grabbing your attention before your feet hit the floor.

Science reveals something fascinating about these early moments. When you first wake up, your brain transitions through different wave states—from delta to theta to alpha waves. Each stage serves a vital purpose in preparing your mind for the day ahead. But when you immediately jump to external stimuli—especially your phone—you force your brain into beta waves, bypassing crucial mental preparation time.[53]

Think of a potter throwing a lump of clay on the wheel. The slightest pressure in those first moments the clay is spinning can mean the difference between a masterpiece and a misshapen vessel. Your morning moments work the same. Your first thoughts, and initial choices, apply subtle pressures that dramatically impact what form your day will take. And once your day begins to take shape, changing course becomes difficult.

Various studies have shown that highly productive people follow morning routines.[54] But it's not just about productivity—it's also about spiritual formation. Just as clay needs to be properly centered on the wheel before it can be shaped, so your soul needs sacred space to align with God's purposes before engaging with the world's demands.

This is an idea that echoes through Scripture. As the prophet Isaiah declared, "You, LORD, are our Father. We are the clay, you are the potter; we are all the work of your hand" (Isaiah 64:8). God desires to be the one who shapes the course of the day—and this comes by following the example of Moses, David, and Jesus himself, who all prioritized those first moments by meeting with God early in the morning.

The question is . . . *Will you do the same?* Will you allow God to shape your day according to his design? Or will you let the world's hurried hands leave you misshapen?

1. Take a moment to consider your specific morning routine. In the table below, write down what you are typically doing in each of the hours indicated after you wake.

Hour after waking	What you are typically doing
First hour	
Second hour	
Third hour	
Fourth hour	

2. One of the objections that people often raise about starting off their day with a quiet time before God is that they are just too busy and there are too many things to do. Read Mark 1:21–39. Jesus had just launched his ministry, and the crowds were pressing in to get his attention. We could say that he was "busy." But why might this have especially compelled him to get up "very early in the morning" and leave that place of chaos to pray? Why do you think Jesus chose "a solitary place" as the location for his time of prayer?

Starting your day by intentionally taking your thoughts captive and setting your mind on what is true, good, lovely, excellent, and praiseworthy (see Philippians 4:8) is the best way to set the course for your thinking. When you start the day by being transformed by the renewing of your mind, it makes it much less likely that you will be conformed to the pattern of this world as the day continues. This is true because of something psychologists call "priming." If you've ever put a coat of primer on a wall before painting it, you know you can't see the primer, but it's there, underneath what you can see. . . . How you choose to start your day "primes" you for the rest of the day to follow.[55]

3. Read Isaiah 43:18–19. One of the ways to "prime" your day is to focus on—to *perceive*—the new things that God is doing in your life. What if—before checking your phone—you started your day by focusing on three "new things" that God is doing in you? How might starting your day actively looking for God's work in your life alter your morning mindset?

4. Turn to Philippians 3:12–14. Think about yesterday's failures, regrets, and missed opportunities. What does it mean for you to "forget" all these things that happened in the past and press on? Read this passage again slowly. What specific burden can you lay down today, knowing that God has a plan for you and wants you to move ahead?

> What it means to "forget" what happened in the past and press on:

What specific burden you can lay down today:

Think about what you say to yourself specifically *in the morning*. You can say, *This is going to be another long day. I have so much to do that I'll never get it all done. I'll probably disappoint people again.* If you do, you will prime your brain, and it may well be the kind of day you have. You'll look for irritations and find them. Remember, that's how confirmation bias works. We set our thoughts, and then our thoughts look for proof and evidence to support them. Or you can start your morning by reminding yourself of God's new mercies and endless compassions and letting your thoughts look for all the ways you can experience his kindness throughout the course of the day.[56]

5. In the early days of modern warfare, artillery units would fire a shot from their cannons, see where it landed, and then adjust the trajectory accordingly to hit their desired target. In the same way, you may need to make adjustments to your morning routine to get the trajectory of your day that you desire. What process do you have in place for evaluating what adjustments you need to make? How have you found that helpful in your morning?

MORNING HEROES

Throughout Scripture, we find an intriguing pattern: The heroes of our faith were early risers. Abraham climbed a mountain at dawn to worship, his feet heavy with the weight of sacrifice. Moses ascended Sinai in the morning light to meet with God. Hannah poured out her heart before the sun rose, her tears mixing with the morning dew. The women rushed to Jesus' tomb as dawn was breaking.

This wasn't mere coincidence or a cultural preference for early rising. These spiritual giants understood something profound about the relationship between time and devotion. They recognized that offering God the first moments of the day was both a practical discipline and a powerful symbol. By rising early, they were making a declaration about their priorities, their dependence, and their dedication.

Consider Daniel's example. In a foreign land, he established a pattern of praying three times daily (see Daniel 6:10)—which is generally interpreted by scholars as meaning he prayed in the morning, at noon, and in the evening. Even under threat of death, Daniel maintained this rhythm, knowing his public courage flowed from his private devotion. In the midst of political pressure and pagan culture, his patterns for prayer remained consistent: windows open toward Jerusalem, knees bent in prayer, heart oriented toward God before engaging with the demands of the palace.

This same theme of "awaking" to God appears in many of the psalms: "Awake, my soul! . . . I will awaken the dawn" (Psalm 57:8). The psalmists saw each sunrise as an opportunity to align their hearts with heaven before facing the earth. Queen Esther, facing a life-or-death mission, called for three days of prayer beginning at dawn. Joshua received his battle strategies in the morning hours. Manna had to be gathered early—a daily lesson in prioritizing divine provision over extra sleep.

This heritage of early rising culminates in Christ, who would slip away to solitary places to pray. The Gospel writers make specific mention of his predawn prayers, his early teaching in the temple, and his morning encounters with seekers and sufferers. If the Son of God prioritized these morning moments with the Father, what does that reveal about our own need? His example stands as an inspiration to understand the impact of giving God our first and best moments.

1. Many heroes of the faith had morning patterns that set the trajectory of their day in a God-given direction. Look up each verse in the table below and write down their actions.

Person	Passage	Morning action
Abraham	Genesis 22:3	
Moses	Exodus 34:4	
Gideon	Judges 6:36–38	
Hezekiah	2 Chronicles 29:20	
Job	Job 1:5	

Life is, in fact, *difficult*. There is such a torrent of negativity that it would be easy to drown in it. Yet we want to live in joy. That's not just what *we* want; it's God's will for our lives. "Rejoice always, pray continually, give thanks in all circumstances; for this is God's will for you in Christ Jesus" (1 Thessalonians 5:16–18). . . . So, how? How do we live with joy in a world that hits us with wave after wave of difficulties? . . . How do find the energy and strength to be present with the people we care about? How do we persevere when life seems too difficult? It starts by *winning the morning*.[57]

2. Every morning, a battle takes place. The choice you face each morning isn't whether to prepare for battle—the battle will come regardless. The choice is whether you will enter it having already surrendered your first moments to God and believe that you can actually *rejoice always*—in any circumstance. What fears, pressures, or demands are you facing right now that make it challenging for you to believe in this truth? (Take those to God in prayer!)

Israel had spent four hundred-plus years as slaves in Egypt, and then they called out to God, asking him to deliver them. God tells them he will free them from slavery and lead them to the land that was promised to them. . . . The Israelites begin their journey out of Egypt toward the promised land, but Pharaoh has a change of heart and sends his armies to pursue them. They are hot on the Israelites' heels, and the Red Sea is looming right in front of the people of Israel. They are trapped. But the people watch as God splits the Red Sea, creating a highway for them to walk through. When the Egyptian army comes after them, the sea collapses on them. As the Israelites continue their journey through the wilderness, God provides for them in undeniably miraculous ways.[58]

3. Read Exodus 16:1–5. One of the ways that God provided for the Israelites was by giving them manna in the wilderness. In doing this, the Lord could have provided a week's worth of manna at once—but he instead chose to provide it *daily*. In what ways do you try to "stockpile" spiritual nourishment rather than seeking God's presence each morning? How might daily spiritual gathering reshape your relationship with him?

4. God used the morning manna as a test of the Israelites' trust in him. What does your morning routine reveal about who or what you trust the most?

5. Read Matthew 6:5–6. Jesus specifically mentions going into a room and closing the door, creating intentional separation from the world's noise. Where is your current "prayer room"? If you don't have one, what small space could you transform into a sacred meeting place with God? What three changes (removing distractions, adding a comfortable chair, creating better lighting) would make this space more conducive to intimate prayer?

Your meeting place with God:

Three changes that would make this space conducive to intimate prayer:

1.

2.

3.

THE DAWN CHORUS

In nature, there's a phenomenon known as the dawn chorus—that magical moment when the birds begin their morning songs, each adding its unique voice to a symphony that welcomes the day. It starts with a single brave call in the darkness and builds as voice after voice joins in . . . until the air itself vibrates with the anticipation of sunrise.

Like these early morning songbirds, our first words have special power to set the tone for all that follows. But for many of us, those early moments are anything but "magical." News alerts on the television scream out what to fear. Social media posts whisper how we don't measure up. Our own internal dialogue hisses yesterday's failures. Instead of joining the dawn chorus of creation, we let these discordant notes dominate our morning symphony.

King David understood the power of first words. He wrote, "In the morning, LORD, you hear my voice; in the morning I lay my requests before you and wait expectantly" (Psalm 5:3). This wasn't mere poetic language—it was a battle strategy for starting his day centered on the Lord. And he wasn't alone. Jeremiah wrote, "Because of the LORD's great love we are not consumed, for his compassions never fail. They are new every morning; great is your faithfulness" (Lamentations 3:22–23). Isaiah added, "The Sovereign LORD . . . wakens me morning by morning, wakens my ear to listen like one being instructed" (Isaiah 50:4).

Again, these weren't just religious rituals or acts of devotion—they were strategic choices about the first words that would shape their day, their destiny, and their legacy. Just as a conductor's opening gesture sets the tempo and tone for the entire symphony, so our morning words conduct the melody of our day. They become the foundation upon which all other words must be built, the key in which our day's song will be sung.

The choice is before us. We can join our voice with the dawn chorus, declaring God's faithfulness before the sun even rises. Or we can let other voices conduct our daily symphony. The decision is ours to make, and it begins with the very first words we speak.

1. In the first personal study, you considered your current morning routine. Now it's time to determine what obstacles, if any, are preventing you from having intentional morning time with God. List three that come to mind, and then provide one possible solution for each.

Obstacle	Possible solution
1.	
2.	
3.	

2. During this week's group time, you were asked, "What would your ideal, God-centered morning routine look like?" Now it's time to get specific about exactly what that would look like. Create a simple morning liturgy—a short sequence of activities you can do that will help you focus yourself on God and win your morning. What three elements would you include in a "perfect" morning plan? How much time would you spend on each? (Don't be so aggressive with your goals that you set yourself up for failure.)

Activity	Time spent
1.	
2.	
3.	

James writes, "Why, you do not even know what will happen tomorrow. What is your life? You are a mist that appears for a little while and then vanishes" (4:14). Now that I think of it, this would be a good thought exercise. Walk into the kitchen or bathroom, wherever you keep the Febreze or the Poo-Pourri (a real thing), and pump a few sprays into the air. You can even hold that trigger down for a whole minute. Then watch how quickly it disappears. James says your life is like that. So why are you spending all your time and energy thinking about the mist and not the things of God?[59]

3. Winning the morning begins with focusing on the things that truly matter—*the things of God*. One of the ways that you can do this is by reminding yourself of God's character and how he feels toward you. The psalms are especially helpful in making such declarations. Look up each of the following verses and write how it could help shape your morning declarations.

Psalm	How this could shape my morning declarations
Psalm 59:16	
Psalm 88:13	
Psalm 90:14	
Psalm 92:1–2	

4. Now take a few minutes to write out some of your own morning declarations. What specific truths could you speak (aloud) the first thing in the morning about the following?

God's character:
Your identity in Christ:
Your purpose for the day:
The promises you are claiming:

We began this study by acknowledging a universal truth—our minds are being molded. Every day, we face an onslaught of thoughts that threaten to conform us to the patterns of this world. . . . But we've also discovered this incredible promise: We are not helpless victims of our thoughts. Through the power of Christ and the renewal of our minds, we can break free from destructive thought patterns and experience true transformation. The challenge before us is great, but so is the promise. . . . The battle for our minds is real, but victory is assured in Christ. The journey of a thousand miles begins with a single step or, in this case, a single thought. *What will yours be?*[60]

5. Consider that last statement: "The journey of a thousand miles begins with a single step or, in this case, a single thought." What steps have you taken during the past five weeks that have proven especially effective in taking your thoughts captive? Who is someone you can share that victory with today?

CONNECT AND DISCUSS

Take time today to connect with a group member and talk about some of the insights from this session. Use any of the prompts below to help guide your discussion.

Which elements of this session about winning the morning—starting your day focusing on God and not the world—spoke to you the most powerfully? Why?

What challenges did you identify in starting your day off by seeking God?

What are some solutions you came up with to change your morning routines in a way that allows you to focus on God the first thing in the morning?

What are some of the morning declarations you made that were impactful?

Who is someone who would benefit from the content in this study? What steps will you take to explore what you have learned with that person?

WRAP IT UP

Use this time to go back and complete any of the study and reflection questions from previous days that you weren't able to finish. Make a note below of any revelations you've had and reflect on any growth or personal insights you've gained.

Talk with your group members about what study you may want to go through together next. Put a date on the calendar for when you will meet again in the future to study God's Word and dive deeper into community.

LEADER'S GUIDE

Thank you for your willingness to lead your group through this study! What you've chosen to do is valuable and will make a difference in the lives of others. *Every Thought Captive* is a five-session Bible study built around video content and small-group inter-action. As the group leader, imagine yourself as the host of a party. Your job is to take care of your guests by managing the details so that when your guests arrive, they can focus on one another and on the interaction around the topic for that session.

Your role as the group leader is not to answer all the questions or reteach the content—the video, book, and study guide will do most of that work. Your job is to guide the experience and cultivate your small group into a connected and en-gaged community. This will make it a place for members to process, question, and reflect—not necessarily to receive more instruction. There are several elements in this leader's guide that will help you as you structure your study and reflection time, so be sure to follow along and take advantage of each one.

BEFORE YOU BEGIN

Before your first meeting, make sure the group members have a copy of this study guide. Alternately, you can hand out the study guides at your first meeting and give the members some time to look over the material and ask any preliminary ques-tions. Also, make sure that the group members are aware that they have access to the streaming videos at any time by following the instructions provided with this guide. During your first meeting, ask the members to provide their names, phone numbers, and email addresses so that you can keep in touch with them.

Generally, the ideal size for a group is eight to ten people, which will ensure that everyone has enough time to participate in discussions. If you have more people, you might want to break up the main group into smaller subgroups. Encourage those who show up at the first meeting to commit to attending the duration of the study, as this will help the group members get to know one another, create stabil-ity for the group, and help you know how best to prepare to lead the participants through the material.

Each session begins with an opening reflection in the Welcome section. The questions that follow in the Connect section serve as icebreakers to get the group members thinking about the session topic. In the rest of the study, it's generally not a good idea to have everyone answer every question—a free-flowing discussion is more desirable. But with the icebreaker question, you can go around the circle and ask each person to respond. Encourage shy people to share, but don't force them.

At your first meeting, let the group members know that each session also contains a personal study section that they can use to continue to engage with the content until the next meeting. While doing this section is optional, it will help participants cement the concepts presented during the group study time and help them better understand how humility will help them see God, themselves, and others more accurately.

Let them know that if they choose to do so, they can watch the video for the next session by accessing the streaming code provided with this study guide. Invite them to bring any questions and insights to your next meeting, especially if they had a breakthrough moment or didn't understand something.

PREPARATION FOR EACH SESSION

As the leader, there are a few things you should do to best prepare for each meeting:

- **Read through the session.** This will help you become more familiar with the content and know how to structure the discussion times.

- **Decide how the videos will be used.** Determine whether you want the members to watch the videos ahead of time or together as a group.

- **Decide which questions you want to discuss.** You may not be able to get through all the questions, so look over the discussion questions provided in each session and mark which ones you definitely want to cover.

- **Be familiar with the questions you want to discuss.** When the group meets, you'll be watching the clock, so be familiar with the questions you selected.

- **Pray for your group.** Pray for your group members and ask God to lead them as they study his Word and listen to his Spirit.

Keep in mind as you lead the discussion time that in many cases there will be no one "right" answer to the questions. Answers will vary, especially when the group members are being asked to share their personal experiences.

STRUCTURING THE DISCUSSION TIME

You will need to determine how long you want your meetings to last so that you can plan your time accordingly. Suggested times for each section have been provided in this guide, and if you adhere to these times, your group will meet for ninety minutes. However, many groups like to meet for two hours. If this describes your particular group, follow the times listed in the right-hand column of the chart given below.

Section	90 Minutes	120 Minutes
CONNECT (discuss one or more of the opening questions for the session)	10 minutes	15 minutes
WATCH (watch the teaching material together and take notes)	25 minutes	25 minutes
DISCUSS (discuss the study questions you selected ahead of time)	35 minutes	50 minutes
RESPOND (write down key takeaways)	10 minutes	15 minutes
PRAY (pray together and dismiss)	10 minutes	15 minutes

As the group leader, it is up to you to keep track of the time and keep things on schedule. You might want to set a timer for each segment so both you and the group members know when the time is up. (There are some good phone apps for timers that play a gentle chime or other pleasant sound instead of a disruptive noise.)

Don't be concerned if group members are quiet or slow to share. People are often quiet when they are pulling together their ideas, and this might be a new experience for some of them. Ask a question and let it hang in the air until someone shares. You can then say, "Thank you. What about others?"

GROUP DYNAMICS

Leading a group through *Every Thought Captive* will prove to be highly rewarding to you and your group members. But you still may encounter challenges along the way! Discussions can get off track. Members may not be sensitive to the needs and ideas of others. Some might worry they will be expected to talk about matters that make them feel awkward. Others may express comments that result in disagreements. To help ease this strain on you and the group, consider the following ground rules:

- When someone raises a question or comment that is off the main topic, suggest you deal with it another time, or, if you feel led to go in that direction, let the group know that you will be spending some time discussing it.

- If someone asks a question that you don't know how to answer, admit it and move on. At your discretion, feel free to invite group members to comment on questions that call for personal experience.

- If you find that one or two people are dominating the discussion time, direct a few questions to others in the group. Outside the main group time, ask the more dominating members to help you draw out the quieter ones. Work to make them part of the solution instead of part of the problem.

- When a disagreement occurs, encourage the group members to process the matter in love. Encourage those on opposite sides to restate what they heard the other side say about the matter, and then invite each side to evaluate if that perception is accurate. Lead the group in examining other Scriptures related to the topic and look for common ground.

When any of these issues arise, encourage your group members to follow these words from Scripture: "Love one another" (John 13:34); "If it is possible, as far as it depends on you, live at peace with everyone" (Romans 12:18); and, "Everyone should be quick to listen, slow to speak and slow to become angry" (James 1:19). This will make your group time more rewarding and beneficial for everyone who attends.

Thank you for taking the time to lead your group through *Every Thought Captive*. You are making a difference in your group members' lives and having an impact on their journey toward a better understanding of how they can take their thoughts captive and experience real transformation in their lives.

NOTES

1. Julie Tseng and Jordan Poppenk, "Brain Meta-state Transitions Demarcate Thoughts Across Task Contexts Exposing the Mental Noise of Trait Neuroticism," *Nature Communications*, no. 11, article 3480 (2020), https://www.nature.com/articles/s41467-020-17255-9#Abs1.
2. Jennice Vilhauer PhD, "How Your Thinking Creates Your Reality," *Psychology Today,* September 21, 2020, https://www.psychologytoday.com/us/blog/living-forward/202009/how-your-thinking-creates-your-reality.
3. Dan Pilat and Sekoul Krastev, "Why Do We Prefer Things That We Are Familiar With?" The Decision Lab, https://thedecisionlab.com/biases/mere-exposure-effect.
4. Lee B. Reid et al., "Interpreting Intervention Induced Neuroplasticity with fMRI: The Case for Multimodal Imaging Strategies," *Neural Plasticity* (2016): 2643491, https://doi.org/10.1155/2016/2643491.
5. Kyle Idleman, *Every Thought Captive: Calm the Mental Chaos That Keeps You Stuck, Drains Your Hope, and Holds You Back* (Grand Rapids, MI: Zondervan, 2025), chapter 2.
6. The Bible says that Satan is "the god of this world" (2 Corinthians 4:4 NLT; see also John 12:31; Ephesians 2:2; Colossians 1:13).
7. Idleman, *Every Thought Captive,* chapter 1.
8. Idleman, *Every Thought Captive,* chapter 2.
9. "List of Best-selling Books," Wikipedia, https://en.wikipedia.org/wiki/List_of_best-selling_books.
10. Rachel Gillett, "Here's How J. K. Rowling Turned Rejection into Unprecedented Success," *Business Insider*, July 20, 2016, https://www.businessinsider.com/how-jk-rowling-turned-rejection-into-success-2016-7.
11. NAS Exhaustive Concordance, Bible Hub, accessed November 12, 2024, https://biblehub.com/hebrew/3820.htm.
12. Idleman, *Every Thought Captive,* chapter 3.
13. Idleman, *Every Thought Captive*, chapter 3.
14. Iman Rastegari and Leah Shafer, "The Biology of Positive Habits," Harvard Graduate School of Education, March 21, 2016, https://www.gse.harvard.edu/ideas/usable-knowledge/16/03/biology-positive-habits.
15. Michael Winnick, "Putting a Finger on Our Phone Obsession," Dscout People Nerds, https://dscout.com/people-nerds/mobile-touches.
16. Simon Kemp, "Digital 2022: Time Spent Using Connected Tech Continues to Rise," Data Reportal, January 26, 2022, https://datareportal.com/reports/digital-2022-time-spent-with-connected-tech.
17. Thayer's and Smith's Bible Dictionary, s.v. "*suschematizo*," accessed January 13, 2025, https://www.biblestudytools.com/lexicons/greek/kjv/suschematizo.html.
18. Idleman, *Every Thought Captive*, section 2.
19. Cambridge Dictionary, s.v. "pattern," https://dictionary.cambridge.org/us/dictionary/english/pattern.
20. Idleman, *Every Thought Captive*, section 3.
21. Ronald Rolheiser, *The Holy Longing: The Search for a Christian Spirituality* (New York: Doubleday, 1999), 32.
22. Idleman, *Every Thought Captive*, chapter 5.
23. Idleman, *Every Thought Captive*, chapter 5.
24. Idleman, *Every Thought Captive*, chapter 4.
25. Idleman, *Every Thought Captive*, chapter 4.
26. See Oliver Burkeman, "The Age of Rage: Are We Really Living in Angrier Times?" *The Guardian*, May 11, 2019, www.theguardian.com/lifeandstyle/2019/may/11/all-fired-up-are-we-really-living-angrier-times.
27. Rodrigo Narvaes and Rosa Maria Martins de Almeida, "Aggressive Behavior and Three Neurotransmitters: Dopamine, GABA, and Serotonin—a Review of the Last 10 Years," APA PsycNet, December 16, 2014, https://psycnet.apa.org/fulltext/2014-56250-020.html.
28. It's important to note that this verse addresses general interpersonal conflicts and minor offenses and is not intended to apply to situations of abuse, severe trauma, or criminal behavior. In such cases, safety is the primary concern, and professional help and/or legal intervention may be necessary. Offense in this context refers to personal slights, misunderstandings, or relational conflicts that don't involve physical, emotional, or spiritual abuse. When approaching any conflict, wisdom, discernment, and sometimes professional guidance are crucial.

The goal is always healing and reconciliation when possible, but not at the expense of anyone's safety. If you're unsure about how to handle a particular situation, seek counsel from a trusted pastor, therapist, or counselor.

29. Idleman, *Every Thought Captive*, chapter 6.
30. Idleman, *Every Thought Captive*, chapter 6.
31. "The Daily Ad Exposure: How Many Ads Does the Average Person See Each Day?" Adfuel Inc., June 27, 2024, https://goadfuel.com/the-daily-ad-exposure-how-many-ads-does-the-average-person-see-each-day/.
32. Idleman, *Every Thought Captive*, chapter 7.
33. Idleman, *Every Thought Captive*, chapter 7.
34. "Long-Term Trends in Deaths of Despair," Joint Economic Committee, September 5, 2019, www.jec.senate.gov/public/index.cfm/republicans/2019/9/long-term-trends-in-deaths-of-despair.
35. "Long-Term Trends in Deaths of Despair," Joint Economic Committee.
36. "Diseases of Despair in the U.S.—Statistics and Facts," Statista, January 8, 2024, https://www.statista.com/topics/5961/diseases-of-despair-in-the-us/#topicOverview.
37. Idleman, *Every Thought Captive*, chapter 8.
38. Idleman, *Every Thought Captive*, chapter 8.
39. Tobias van Schneider, "If You Want It, You Might Get It: The Reticular Activating System Explained," Medium, June 22, 2017, https://medium.com/desk-of-van-schneider/if-you-want-it-you-might-get-it-the-reticular-activating-system-explained-761b6ac14e53.
40. "Can Gratitude Improve Quality of Life?" Princeton Health News, November 22, 2022, https://www.princetonhcs.org/about-princeton-health/news-and-information/news/can-gratitude-increase-quality-of-life.
41. Thomas W. Hodo et al., "Critical Neurotransmitters in the Neuroimmune Network," *Frontiers in Immunology* 11 (2020), https://doi.org/10.3389/fimmu.2020.01869.
42. Srini Pillay, MD, "Why You Can't Get a Song out of Your Head and What to Do About It," Harvard Health Publishing, October 4, 2017, https://www.health.harvard.edu/blog/why-you-cant-get-a-song-out-of-your-head-and-what-to-do-about-it-2017100412490.
43. Victoria J. Williamson et al., "Sticky Tunes: How Do People React to Involuntary Musical Imagery?" *PLOS One* 9, no. 1 (2014): e86170, https://doi.org/10.1371/journal.pone.0086170.
44. Pillay, "Why You Can't Get a Song out of Your Head and What to Do About It."
45. Idleman, *Every Thought Captive*, chapter 11.
46. Idleman, *Every Thought Captive*, chapter 11.
47. Idleman, *Every Thought Captive*, chapter 11.
48. Idleman, *Every Thought Captive*, chapter 11.
49. Idleman, *Every Thought Captive*, chapter 9.
50. Idleman, *Every Thought Captive*, chapter 9.
51. Jay Rai, "Why You Should Stop Checking Your Phone in the Morning (and What to Do Instead)," *Forbes*, April 2, 2021, www.forbes.com/sites/forbescoachescouncil/2021/04/02/why-you-should-stop-checking-your-phone-in-the-morning-and-what-to-do-instead/.
52. Alvin Powell, "Soothing Advice for Mad America," *Harvard Gazette*, August 14, 2020, https://news.harvard.edu/gazette/story/2020/08/a-closer-look-at-americas-pandemic-fueled-anger.
53. Rai, "Why You Should Stop Checking Your Phone in the Morning (and What to Do Instead)."
54. Amantha Imber, "What Super Productive People Do Differently," Harvard Business Review, December 8, 2020, https://hbr.org/2020/12/what-super-productive-people-do-differently.
55. Idleman, *Every Thought Captive*, chapter 12.
56. Idleman, *Every Thought Captive*, chapter 12.
57. Idleman, *Every Thought Captive*, chapter 12.
58. Idleman, *Every Thought Captive*, chapter 10.
59. Idleman, *Every Thought Captive*, chapter 13.
60. Idleman, *Every Thought Captive*, chapter 13.

ABOUT THE
AUTHOR

Kyle Idleman is the senior pastor at Southeast Christian Church in Louisville, Kentucky, one of the largest churches in America. On a normal weekend, he speaks to more than thirty thousand people spread across fourteen campuses. More than anything else, Kyle enjoys unearthing the teachings of Jesus and making them relevant in people's lives. He is a frequent speaker for national conventions and influential churches across the country. Kyle and his wife, DesiRae, have been married for over thirty years. They have four children, two sons-in-law, and recently welcomed their third grandchild. They live on a farm in Kentucky, where he doesn't do any actual farming. For more information, visit www.kyleidleman.com.